CW01468763

SAMUEL SLANEY

The Hybrid 8.5

Football's Evolving Midfield Role

This book was professionally typeset on Reedsy.
Find out more at reedsy.com

Contents

A Note to the Reader

Hi, I'm Samuel Slaney, and I'm grateful you took the opportunity to get this book. What you're about to discover has the potential to completely reshape how you see the game — not just from the stands or the sidelines, but from deep within the heart of the pitch. This is more than just a book. It's a tactical awakening.

Since 2018, I've been immersed in the world of football performance, analysis, and tactical development — not just as a fan or observer, but as a student of the game. I hold a Master of Science degree in Football Analysis, and over the years, I've worked inside elite academy systems. Additionally. through years of independent research, writing, and practical observation, I've explored the game's tactical evolution in depth.

Through this journey, I've witnessed first-hand how modern football has evolved, and continues to evolve — and how many frameworks and methods for understanding the game have struggled to keep pace. Nowhere is this more obvious than in the evolution of midfield roles.

The traditional models no longer explain what's unfolding on the pitch. The rise of the Hybrid 8.5 reflects a deeper shift — one that demands new thinking, clearer structures, and a fresh lens through which to view the modern game.

That's why this book was written. To bring clarity. To close the gap. And to redefine what's possible for coaches, analysts, players, and passionate students of the sport alike.

After all, maybe you've spent hours watching matches, reading blogs, or listening to podcasts — and yet still feel like something's missing. You can see the movement, the patterns, the transitions... but you can't quite piece it all together. The terminology feels vague. The roles blur. And the deeper you go, the more overwhelming it becomes. You want to understand the game at a tactical level, but it's like trying to solve a puzzle with pieces from three different boxes.

Maybe you've tried to apply what you've learned to your coaching sessions, your analysis reports, or your own game on the pitch — only to find it doesn't quite translate. The insights are too generic. The frameworks too outdated. You look for modern solutions, but all you find are recycled ideas from a decade ago. You're searching for clarity, but all you get is noise.

Or maybe you've even bought book after book, hoping to find that one breakthrough concept... only to discover it's just another rehash of what you already know. The same names. The same formations. The same surface-level analysis dressed up as something new. And you're left wondering — *is there anyone actually talking about what's really happening in the modern game?*

The truth is, you're not alone. It seems most are becoming a victim of the outdated tactical models that haven't evolved with the game. They're trying to understand the modern midfielder through a framework that was built for a different era. And it's holding them back.

That feeling of frustration. Confusion. Even self-doubt. Like you're missing something obvious — some invisible thread that connects it all. You've got the passion. You've got the hunger. But you're stuck in a loop of half-insights and dead ends.

Here's what most don't realise... The Hybrid 8.5 isn't just a trend. It's a tactical nuance of modern football. It's what separates the elite from the average. The players who dictate the game from those who chase shadows. And without a clear understanding of this evolution, you'll always be one step behind.

And now with the possibility of AI-driven scouting, data-informed coaching, and systems-based playing philosophies becoming the norm — if you're not ahead of the tactical curve, you're not even in the conversation. The game is moving fast. And it won't wait for you to catch up.

It seems most are left in a state of tactical paralysis — watching the game play out, sensing there's something deeper happening, but not having the tools to decode it. And that's a dangerous place to be. Because if you can't see the shifts, you can't adapt. If you can't adapt, you can't evolve. And if you can't evolve... then sooner or later, you're out of the game. Whether you're a coach, a player, or a student of the sport — you risk becoming irrelevant in a game that's leaving behind those who refuse to see it differently.

Introduction

There's a moment in every match — just a few seconds, often overlooked, barely mentioned in post-match coverage — when the entire tempo of play shifts. Not because of a thunderous tackle or a gravity-defying goal, but because one player, standing in the vortex between chaos and control, found the invisible pass. A turn, a touch, a pass that breaks two lines. The crowd might not gasp. The commentator might not even flinch. But those who know — the coaches, the analysts, the players who live in the details — they see it. They feel it.

You're here because you've seen it too. Maybe you couldn't name it before, but you recognised it. You've sensed there's a role emerging in modern football — an unlabelled position that doesn't conform to the traditional numbers. Not quite an 8, not quite a 10. Something in between. Something more.

This is the 8.5.

And if you're serious about understanding where football is going — not just formations on a tactics board, but how those formations breathe, morph, and adapt in real time — then mastering this role is non-negotiable. Whether you're a coach trying to evolve your system, a player searching for the edge, or a fan obsessed with the chess match beneath the surface, the 8.5 is the lens that reframes it all.

What follows is not a romanticised memoir or a nostalgic look at the *'good old days'*. This is a field manual for the future of football — a deep dive into the most tactically transformative role in the modern game. But before we talk systems, drills, or data, let's start with the why. Why this matters. Why the 8.5 is reshaping everything from the academy pitch to the Champions League final. And why, if you care about football in its purest and most advanced form, this is the role you need to understand.

The Middle is Where the Game Lives

You've probably heard it said a thousand times: football is won and lost in midfield. But that quote is outdated. Too vague. The truth is sharper — **football is shaped in midfield**. The outcome might be decided in the box, but the identity of a team is forged in the centre of the pitch. It's where tempo is dictated, where pressing traps are triggered, and where attacking moves are born before they're even noticed.

But not all midfielders are created equal. And here's where it gets interesting.

In the past, roles were clearly defined. The 6 sat deep and shielded. The 10 floated behind the striker, pulling strings. The 8 ran box-to-box, the ever-reliable engine. But as pressing got smarter, spaces tighter, and build-ups more intricate, these neat categories began to blur. Teams needed players who could do more — who could connect, adapt, and anticipate across multiple phases. Not just specialists, but hybrids.

That's where you come in. If you're a coach, you're looking for players who can read multiple pictures at once — who can be a controller, a disruptor, and a creator within the same 90 minutes. If you're a player, you're chasing that rare edge — the ability to affect the game in every third without losing your identity. And if you're an analyst or a purist, you're tracking how this evolution is being written not in headlines, but in heat maps, pass networks, and off-ball movements.

The 8.5 lives in that evolution. It's not a trend. It's the tactical spine of the modern game.

Tactical Literacy is the New Superpower

In an era where every team has access to video, data, and analysis, the biggest differentiator is not information — it's interpretation. Tactical literacy has become football's new superpower. The players who thrive aren't always the fastest or the strongest. They're the ones who see the game four passes ahead.

The 8.5 is built for this era.

This role doesn't just demand technical ability — it demands cognitive sharpness. The ability to scan under pressure, to understand triggers, to manipulate space without touching the ball. You're no longer just reacting to the game — you're shaping it.

Think of the best teams in the world over the last five years. What do they have in common? **Fluidity. Interchangeability. Central control**. Whether it's Manchester City building triangles on the edge of the box, Liverpool collapsing the midfield to spring a counter, or Spain's youth systems producing metronomes in boots — the 8.5 is often the hidden conductor.

And here's the thing most people miss: tactical intelligence isn't innate. It's trainable. It's coachable. It's a skillset that can be broken down, refined, and redeployed. That's what makes this role so powerful. You're not waiting for a generational talent to emerge. You're building one through design, not luck.

As a coach, it means rethinking your drills. As a player, it means redefining your training. As an analyst, it means shifting your lens from outcome to process. Because the 8.5 isn't about flashy numbers. It's about invisible influence. And once you learn to see it, you'll never unsee it.

The Role that Redefines Roles

The 8.5 doesn't replace the 8 or the 10. It reimagines them. It's the role that redefines roles.

You know how some players seem to always be in the right place — not just to receive the ball, but to make something happen? They don't chase the play. They shape it. They create passing angles, stretch defensive lines, and trigger overloads without even touching the ball. That's not instinct. That's intentional. That's the 8.5 blueprint.

This role exists in the half-spaces, between the lines, in the moments when systems momentarily collapse and someone has to impose order. It's the most tactically demanding role on the pitch because it requires you to live in flux. One moment you're supporting the pivot, the next you're ghosting into the box. **You defend like a six, create like a ten, and transition like an eight.** This isn't a luxury role. It's a necessity.

If you're a coach, imagine having a player who can switch your shape mid-possession without a touchline signal. If you're a player, think about what it means to be indispensable — to be the one who links it all together. Not the loudest, but the most essential.

The best part? You don't need to be the flashiest. You need to be the smartest. The most adaptable. The one who turns systems into solutions.

And that's why this matters.

Because this isn't about tactics for tactics' sake. It's about unlocking a deeper understanding of the game you love. It's about seeing football not just as a sport, but as an interconnected system of patterns, decisions, and roles that evolve faster than the commentary can keep up with.

When you master the 8.5, you don't just learn a position. You learn how to see the game differently. You learn how top managers think, how elite players train, and how modern systems thrive.

And once you step into that understanding, you don't just watch football. You interpret it. You decode it. You influence it.

Welcome to the future of midfield. Welcome to the 8.5.

1

Origins of the 8.5: Where the Game Changed

The Classical Midfield Trinity

The 6, 8, and 10 Roles Defined

Before the diagrams, data dashboards, and drone footage, football was already deeply structured—just not in the way we map it today. The midfield, often referred to as the *"engine room,"* has always been central to a team's rhythm. But what exactly did that engine look like in its original form?

Let's rewind. In the traditional midfield trio, each number told its own story. The number 6? The sentinel. He sat deep, often just ahead of the centre-backs, and was tasked with shielding the defence, breaking up attacks, and recycling possession. Claude Makélélé made the 6 his own, so much so that the role was literally renamed after him in certain coaching circles. He didn't score screamers or dribble past five men. He did something rarer—he made others better by doing less, brilliantly.

The number 8? The box-to-box dynamo. This role was about perpetual motion. Think Steven Gerrard in his prime—surging runs, last-ditch tackles, and the occasional 30-yard thunderbolt. The 8 was the bridge, the connector, the heartbeat that kept the pulse steady between defence and attack.

And then there was the number 10. The artist. Positioned just behind the striker, the 10 existed in a world of his own—floating in pockets of space, threading impossible passes, changing games with a flick or a glance. Zinedine Zidane, Francesco Totti, Juan Román Riquelme—these players defined an era where individual flair could dictate collective fate.

Each role was distinct. Each had its own zone of influence. And for a long time, football respected these boundaries.

Historical Formations and Midfield Distribution

To understand these roles in context, you need to look at how teams were laid out in earlier tactical eras. Consider the 4-4-2, the foundation of English football from the late 20th century through to the early 2000s. Two central midfielders shared responsibilities—one more defensive, the other more progressive. There was little room for a true 10. Creativity often came from wide players or clever strikers dropping deep.

In contrast, the 4-3-1-2 and the Brazilian 4-2-2-2 embraced the 10. These systems created a natural space for a playmaker to operate behind two forwards, supported by a double pivot. You'd often see deep-lying creators like Andrea Pirlo paired with destroyers like Gennaro Gattuso, enabling a player like Kaká to roam freely ahead.

2

The Dutch Total Football of the 1970s, led by Rinus Michels and personified by Johan Cruyff, disrupted static roles. Midfielders interchanged positions constantly, but even then, the numbers still held meaning. The 6 stayed deeper, the 8 carried through zones, the 10 worked between the lines.

The point is: historical formations were built around defined roles. Coaches and players respected spatial hierarchy. There was order. And then, slowly, chaos crept in—but a creative, tactical kind of chaos.

Early Innovators of Positional Play

The line between structure and improvisation began to blur with the rise of positional play—or *"juego de posición"* as it's known in its spiritual home of Spain. This wasn't just about where players stood; it was about where they should be relative to teammates, opponents, and the ball—at all times.

One of the earliest pioneers was Johan Cruyff at Barcelona in the late '80s and early '90s. His 3-4-3 demanded midfielders who could think geometrically—occupying space rather than chasing the ball. Pep Guardiola, then a young pivot in that system, absorbed this philosophy like a sponge.

Fast-forward to Guardiola's own managerial career, and you see the full evolution. At Barcelona, Bayern Munich, and Manchester City, he's redefined the midfield. His teams often abandon traditional numbering altogether. Instead of a rigid 6-8-10 setup, you'll see a *"false 6,"* an *"inverted 8,"* or a *"free 8"* who drifts into the half-space, connects play, and presses high—all in one phase of play.

But Pep wasn't alone. Marcelo Bielsa, the godfather of

3

intensity, demanded verticality and fluidity. Arsène Wenger's Invincibles used midfielders like Patrick Vieira and Gilberto Silva who could both destroy and create. José Mourinho, in his early Chelsea days, used Frank Lampard as a late-arriving 8 who scored like a forward but tracked back like a soldier.

These innovators didn't just tinker with systems—they manipulated time and space. They asked a simple but radical question: **Why should a midfielder be only one thing?**

The *answer*, increasingly, was: **they shouldn't.**

And that's where the door opened for what we now call the 8.5.

That hybrid role was born not in a single moment, but through the accumulation of tactical experimentation. It emerged as football's answer to a world that was speeding up, squeezing space, and demanding more from its players.

The classical trinity of 6-8-10 still exists in coaching manuals. But on the pitch, the lines are blurred. And in that blur, the 8.5 emerged—not as a replacement, but as a response.

A response to pressing systems that suffocate time on the ball. A response to formations that morph mid-possession. A response to the need for midfielders who can defend like a 6, carry like an 8, and create like a 10—all within the same passage of play.

You don't just find the 8.5 in tactics boards or heatmaps. You see it in the way Ilkay Gündoğan ghosts into scoring positions under Guardiola. You see it in how Jude Bellingham breaks lines with the ball, then presses like a terrier after losing it. You saw it in Frank Lampard before we had the language to call it what it is.

What began as a trinity has become a spectrum. And somewhere in the middle—between control and chaos, between

4

defence and attack, between the past and the future—you find the 8.5.

Tactical Shifts of the 21st Century

"The midfield is where the game is won, lost, and rewritten." – Modern coaching adage found scribbled in the margins of a scout's notebook somewhere in La Masia, circa 2008.

Football didn't change overnight. It never does. What happens instead is a slow, tectonic shift—sometimes subtle, sometimes seismic—that only becomes obvious once the dust has settled. This is especially true in midfield, the area of the pitch that often acts as the canary in the tactical coal mine. If you want to know how the game is evolving, watch the midfielders. They'll always tell you first.

The Fall of the Traditional Number 10

In the early 2000s, you still had the classic Number 10 pulling strings behind a striker. Zidane, Riquelme, Kaká—artists in boots. They operated in the mythical *"hole"* between midfield and defence, a zone that, for a while, was sacred. Managers built systems around them. The 4-2-3-1 was essentially a shrine to the ten.

But then came the pressing.

Teams stopped letting the ten breathe. Defensive midfielders began hunting in pairs. Space evaporated. The luxury role became an endangered species, and many of the game's most technically gifted players suddenly found themselves without a natural habitat.

5

Take Mesut Özil. At his peak, he was the quintessential creator. But as pressing systems tightened, and defensive structures dropped deeper, he became easier to isolate. Managers started to ask: *can he run? Can he press? Can he recover?*

The answer, too often, was no.

As the game became faster, less forgiving, and more transitional, the classic ten was forced to evolve or disappear. Some dropped deeper. Others were redeployed wide. Some became eights. And a few—only a few—became something new entirely.

Rise of the Double Pivot and Pressing

To understand why the ten faded, you need to understand what replaced them. Enter the double pivot.

This tactical feature, most commonly seen in a 4-2-3-1 or 4-4-2 diamond, was a response to the demands of control. Managers wanted to dominate the middle, both in and out of possession. Having two midfielders sit in front of the back line gave teams stability, protection, and a launchpad for possession cycles.

Think of Xabi Alonso and Sergio Busquets in Spain's 2012 Euros-winning side. Or Schweinsteiger and Khedira for Germany in 2014. These weren't just defensive midfielders—they could pass, break lines, and resist pressure. The double pivot became the antidote to chaos.

But it was also a tactical statement. By fielding two deeper midfielders, you were signalling that your central structure mattered more than flair. The creative burden shifted. Now, full-backs overlapped with more freedom. Wingers tucked inside. False nines dropped deep. Creation became a collective task.

At the same time, pressing took centre stage. Managers like Jürgen Klopp, Marcelo Bielsa, and Ralph Hasenhüttl began deploying high-energy, trigger-based press systems that turned the middle third into a battlefield. The transitional moments—those five seconds after a turnover—became more important than structured possession.

To survive in this environment, midfielders needed to be tactically sharp, physically robust, and positionally versatile. The game no longer tolerated passengers.

So, what happened to the creative players who didn't fit the mould of a six or a pure eight? They didn't vanish. They adapted. They became hybrids.

Influence of Possession-Based Systems

While some teams leaned into pressing and verticality, others doubled down on control. Guardiola's Barcelona may not have invented possession football, but they certainly rebranded it. Suddenly, everyone wanted a *"third man,"* everyone talked about *"triangles,"* and rondos became more than just warm-ups—they were philosophy in motion.

In these systems, the midfield became a zone of perpetual movement and recalibration. The six acted as a metronome. The eights became circulators and half-space operators. And the lines between roles began to blur.

What made Barça's midfield of Busquets, Xavi, and Iniesta so revolutionary wasn't their individual brilliance—it was their collective intelligence. They moved as if tethered by invisible string, constantly adjusting to maintain balance and superiority.

This model spread. Bayern, Man City, Ajax, and even national teams like Spain and Germany began to adopt variations of it. The midfield became more interconnected, more fluid. Players could no longer be categorised by static numbers. They had to be multifunctional.

Possession-based systems demanded vertical and horizontal connectivity. You couldn't just be good in your own zone—you had to be good in multiple zones. That's where the hybrid role began to form. A player who could link play like an eight, create like a ten, press like a false nine, and recover like a six.

Not many players could do it. But the ones who could started to define the game.

You started seeing players like Kevin De Bruyne, who blurred the lines between creator and box-to-box engine. Or Ilkay Gündoğan, who drifted into advanced areas at will, arriving late in the box but also dropping into the build-up. These weren't tens. They weren't eights. They were something in between— something new.

In Italy, Nicolo Barella began to emerge as a prototype of the modern midfielder. Constantly in motion, shuttling from box to box, threading passes, and pressing with intent. In Germany, Leon Goretzka brought power, timing, and technique in equal measure. These were midfielders who belonged in systems that demanded everything—and gave nothing for free.

The shift wasn't just tactical, it was philosophical. Coaches began to see the midfield not as a place of specialists, but of connectors. Players who could bridge ideas, phases, and positions. The 8.5 wasn't born in a formation—it was born in a need. A need to adapt, to survive, and to optimise.

The tactical shifts of the 21st century didn't just change the shape of the midfield—they changed its function. Systems became less about where you start, and more about what problems you solve. **The 8.5 isn't a role you assign; it's a role you earn by being indispensable in the spaces that decide games.**

Look at the next time you watch a top-level match. Focus on the midfielders floating between the lines. Not quite a ten, not quite an eight. Watch how they interpret space, how they rotate with teammates, how they accelerate the tempo. That's the modern game's most valuable currency: adaptability in motion.

And it all started when the game stopped waiting for Number Tens to make something happen—and started demanding that midfielders make everything happen.

The Birth of the Hybrid 8.5

There's a moment in every tactical revolution where the lines start to blur—literally. On a whiteboard, the 8 and 10 used to sit in neat, separate boxes. The 8 was the industrious link, the box-to-box soldier. The 10 was the artist, floating behind the striker, pulling strings. But as football evolved, so did the spaces in between. The 8.5 isn't just a player—it's the product of tactical necessity and creative defiance, born out of systems that demanded more than tradition could provide.

Blurring Lines Between The 8 and 10

To understand the emergence of the 8.5, you need to look at what was missing. Football, in its iterative genius, tends to solve problems by hybridising roles. Too much distance between the pivot and the playmaker? Enter the player who can do both. You watched teams trying to press high, only to get bypassed by midfielders who could operate in that grey area between creation and control.

The classical 8 and 10 had limitations. The 8 could shuttle and support, sure, but rarely did they consistently unlock defences in tight pockets. The 10, on the other hand, often lacked the defensive engine or positional discipline to contribute without the ball. The 8.5 emerged as the answer not by design, but by evolution. Coaches stopped asking, *"Is he a 10 or an 8?"* and started asking, *"Can he do both?"*

The defining trait of the 8.5 isn't technical flair or tactical discipline—it's the ability to transition between roles without friction. One minute they're making a third-man run into the box; the next, they're dropping beside the pivot to overload a build-up phase. You're not watching two players—you're watching one who can be both without the seams showing.

Watch players like İlkay Gündoğan at his peak under Guardiola, or Jude Bellingham's evolution across Dortmund and Madrid. These aren't players who fit into neat boxes. They float, they slide, they adjust. They're not caught between identities—they've created a new one.

Demands of Fluid Systems

As possession-based systems began to dominate, the rigidity of fixed midfield roles became a liability. Positional play—or juego de posición, if we're being purist—did more than change formations. It redefined what space meant. Suddenly, zones were dynamic, not fixed. Your role wasn't just about where you started, but where you moved based on the ball, your teammates, and the opposition's structure.

In these systems, the 8.5 became essential. You needed someone who could occupy the half-space in possession, drop into a double pivot when defending deep, and still arrive late in the box to finish a move. That's not a traditional profile—it's a Frankenstein-esque monster of midfield excellence, stitched together by necessity and ambition.

Coaches started designing shapes that begged for this kind of player. Think of the 4-3-3 morphing into a 3-2-5 in possession. Suddenly, the interior midfielder wasn't just supporting the attack—he was the fulcrum around which rotations happened. The 8.5 had to understand when to push, when to hold, and how to manipulate space without ever being static.

It wasn't about being everywhere—it was about being exactly where the game needed you. That's what fluid systems demand: not more movement, but smarter movement.

You saw it in the way teams began to build their attacks. Full-backs tucked inside, wingers stayed high and wide, and the 8.5 found the pockets that opened up in between. In a world where defenders were trained to watch the ball, the 8.5 became the ghost in the machine—never the obvious option, but always the devastating one.

11

Emergence of Transitional Midfielders

The modern game lives in the margins—the milliseconds between losing the ball and winning it back, the metres between a compact block and a stretched line. Transitional phases became the currency of control, and the 8.5 emerged as the trader fluent in both sides of the market.

Unlike traditional midfielders who had fixed roles in attack or defence, the 8.5 thrives in ambiguity. They don't just react to transitions—they anticipate them. Before a pass is made, they're already positioning for the next phase. That's what sets them apart. It's not about being reactive; it's about being proactive in chaos.

You'll notice it in how they press. Not like a headless presser lunging forward, but as a trigger-based operator who understands the chain reaction of spatial compression. They press not just to win the ball, but to manipulate where the ball will go next.

Then there's their ability to flip the field in seconds. Win the ball in midfield? They don't play safe. They carry, they commit defenders, they create overloads. It's not just about counter-attacking—it's about counter-constructing. They turn a defensive moment into an attacking structure before the opposition has even reset.

Think of players like Federico Valverde at Real Madrid—a player who can charge 40 metres with a carry, arrive in the box, and still cover the flank if the full-back has bombed forward. That's not a box-to-box midfielder in the traditional sense. That's a transitional technician, someone who thrives in the in-between moments where games are won or lost.

This kind of player forces a rethink of training methodology.

You can't coach the 8.5 in isolated drills. You need to simulate chaos. Situational rondos, compressed space transitions, and phase-based pattern play—these are the environments where the 8.5 is forged.

What you're seeing is the rise of a role that doesn't just survive in modern football. It defines it. The 8.5 is the player who fills the gaps that systems create, the glue between possession and progression, the first attacker and the final defender. Not by accident. By design.

And the game is only just beginning to catch up.

2

Why the 8.5 Matters: The Neural Network of Modern Football

The Connective Tissue of the Pitch

Here's the uncomfortable truth: most fans still watch football in straight lines. Defenders defend, attackers attack, and midfielders hustle somewhere in between. But when you start watching the game with an analytical lens, or better yet, when you coach or play within a tactical framework, you realise that the most important roles often occupy the grey space — the zones between structure and spontaneity, between phases of play, and between the lines. The 8.5 lives there.

This hybrid midfielder isn't just another cog in the machine. They are the neural network that links everything together. Not quite a playmaker, not quite a box-to-box runner, and not a destroyer either. The 8.5 is the hinge. And nowhere is that more evident than in the way they bind a team vertically, stretch it horizontally, and manipulate space with the subtlety of a chess grandmaster.

Vertical Connectivity Between Defence and Attack

You've heard the clichés: *"Play through the thirds," "Break lines," "Link the back to the front."* But what does this actually look like when done well?

Watch Kevin De Bruyne drop just inside his own half. He's not tracking back — he's recalibrating. One scan over his shoulder, a touch to set the tempo, and he fires a pass between two midfield lines with such precision you could draw it with a compass. That's verticality — not just kicking it forward but connecting zones of the pitch with intent.

The 8.5 isn't waiting for the ball to come to them. They're dictating where the next connection will be. In teams that build from the back, their job is to offer the first meaningful vertical pass option after the pivot. They're not the deepest, but they are often the most available. That availability doesn't come from standing still — it comes from reading body shapes, anticipating passing lanes, and appearing in space just as the centre-back opens their body. Timing is everything.

In more direct systems, the 8.5 becomes a second-wave option. When the ball is played long or wide, they're the one arriving to receive the knockdown, recycle possession, or drive the next phase. In both styles, they're the bridge between the bricks.

Horizontal Balance and Overloads

You've probably heard coaches scream *"Switch it!"* more times than you can count. That's because horizontal imbalance — pulling the opponent from side to side — is one of the oldest ways to create space. But switching play isn't just about full-backs pinging diagonal balls. It's about using players like the 8.5 to shift the opponent's internal compass.

Think about the rhythm of a good DJ. Peaks and troughs, fast transitions, slow builds. A great 8.5 manages the rhythm of a team's horizontal shape in the same way. They show wide when the full-back is pinned, come narrow when the winger is isolated, and swap zones with the pivot or attacking midfielder to stretch the midfield line. Their movement forces defenders into decisions — follow and risk opening a channel, or hold and concede ground.

In systems like Guardiola's 3-2-5, it's common to see the 8.5 step into wide half-spaces, combining with inverted full-backs or wingers to create numerical superiority. It's not about traditional width; it's about occupying uncomfortable spaces — the zones between the 6 and the 8, or between the 8 and the 10. These are the pockets where matches are won, not by flashy skills, but by subtle overloads and intelligent positioning.

The real genius? They do this without breaking the team's shape. They know when to rotate, when to hold, and most importantly, when to vacate space to let others thrive. That level of spatial awareness isn't instinctive. It's trained. It's coached. And it's rare.

Spatial Manipulation

Here's where things get really interesting. The best 8.5s don't just move into space — they move defenders out of it. They manipulate.

Watch Ilkay Gündoğan in his prime City days. He floats into

innocuous zones, drawing a marker ever so slightly. That marker's movement creates a cascading effect — the pivot shifts to cover, the centre-back adjusts his stance, and suddenly, the No. 9 has a passing lane. Gündoğan may not even touch the ball in that sequence, but he's authored the moment.

This is spatial manipulation. It's the tactical equivalent of a feint — not with the ball, but with positioning. It's the 8.5's superpower.

They understand that football is a game of space more than it is a game of possession. By dragging markers, underlapping instead of overlapping, and timing late arrivals rather than early sprints, they reshape the map of the pitch without needing the ball.

This is why traditional statistics miss their influence. You won't always find them leading in key passes or distance covered. But watch the tape. They're the reason the key pass even existed. They're the gravity that pulls the defence out of orbit.

Spatial manipulation also shows up in transitional moments. When possession is won, the 8.5 knows whether to drive forward or hold. When the ball is lost, they know whether to press or delay. Their spatial decisions control the tempo of the game like a metronome.

The elite ones — think Luka Modrić, Frenkie de Jong — they don't just see the space that's open. They see the space that will be open in three seconds. That anticipatory edge separates the competent from the world-class.

Why This Matters

If you're a coach, you already know that most tactical break-downs happen in transition. The 8.5 is the insurance policy against chaos. They're the player who senses when to fill in for a vacated full-back, when to slow down an attack to allow the block to reset, or when to surge forward to exploit an unbalanced opponent.

If you're a player, developing this connective role means mastering the art of invisibility. You'll rarely be the highlight reel. But you'll be the reason the clips exist. It's about knowing the angles before the pass is played, reading defenders like a poker player reads a bluff, and **always — always — scanning.**

And if you're an analyst or enthusiast, start watching matches through this lens. Watch not where the ball is, but where the 8.5 is. When did they move? Who followed? What chain reaction did it cause? That's the neural network at work.

The 8.5 doesn't just connect passes. They connect intention to execution. They make the system breathe.

And when they do it right, the game looks effortless.

Tactical Flexibility and Intelligence

The hybrid 8.5 doesn't just play football — they interpret it. Like a jazz musician who knows when to riff and when to hold a note, the 8.5 thrives in the space between instruction and improvisation. They're not just hardwired into a tactical blueprint; they're the editor, the translator, and sometimes the disruptor. If the midfield is the brain of the team, the 8.5 is the synapse — constantly firing, constantly adjusting, constantly learning. To understand the true value of the 8.5, you need to dive into their ability to read, react, and reshape the game in real time.

Let's get into the mechanics of that footballing intelligence.

Reading Multiple Game Phases

The 8.5 operates across more phases of play than any other position. That isn't just a claim; it's backed by how elite teams track player involvement across build-up, progression, final third entries, pressing, and defensive transitions. The 8.5 shows up in all of them — and not as a passenger.

What separates a good midfielder from a game-changer is the ability to read what phase the game is in and recalibrate their decision-making accordingly. Is the team in stable possession? The 8.5 positions themselves to create a numerical advantage in midfield. Is the team in transition? They either sprint into open space to receive the first forward pass or drop to provide a safety valve. Has possession been lost? They're already scanning to identify the nearest press trigger or cover zone.

This is not instinct. It's trained perception. The 8.5 is constantly scanning not just for the ball, but for spatial cues: how many players are committed forward, how compact the opposition is, where the nearest opposition midfielder is turning. That constant recalibration is what allows them to be one second ahead in a sport where one second is the difference between threading the needle and being countered.

You'll often hear coaches talk about *"game rhythm"* — the tempo and balance of phases within a match. The 8.5 is the metronome. They're not just reacting to the rhythm; they're

19

setting it.

Adapting Shape Mid-Play

Formations are static. Football is not. The real game exists between the numbers on the tactics board.

The 8.5 is key to a team's ability to morph its shape during live play without a single instruction from the touchline. Think of those moments when a full-back inverts into midfield and suddenly the team is in a 3-2-5. Or when a winger tucks in and the 8.5 shifts wide to maintain width. These are not rehearsed set pieces; they're live, evolving patterns that require high-level spatial awareness and decision-making.

The 8.5 adapts by reading the triggers: a teammate's movement, an overload on the flank, an opponent stepping out of shape. The best 8.5s don't wait for instruction — they act, and the team follows. It's why coaches obsessively watch them in training: not just their technique, but their ability to *"feel"* the team's shape and adjust in the moment.

This ability to morph shape mid-play has huge implications. It stretches opponents, creates temporary mismatches, and disrupts pressing structures. When a team can shift organically during live play, it becomes unpredictable. And unpredictability is tactical oxygen.

There's an old coaching phrase: *"Your shape without the ball is your castle. Your shape with the ball is your canvas."* The 8.5 is both the architect and the painter.

Role-Switching and Interchangeability

In elite football, positional play isn't about being in a fixed location — it's about occupying zones with purpose. The 8.5 excels because they're not bound to a single zone. They float, rotate, and switch roles depending on what the game demands.

This role-switching isn't just a clever trick. It's essential to modern systems that rely on positional rotations to destabilise opponents. One minute the 8.5 is supporting the single pivot in the build-up, the next minute they're in the right half-space drawing out a centre-back, then ghosting into the box like a late-arriving No. 10. These movements are more than creative expression — they force defensive recalibration.

But here's the crucial bit: it only works if it's synchronised. The 8.5 must have a deep understanding of their teammates' roles and responsibilities. When they rotate out of position, someone must rotate in. The triangle always has to be preserved. It's like jazz, yes — but jazz played by musicians who know exactly when to come in on the beat. There's freedom, but it's structured freedom.

And this is where tactical intelligence becomes non-negotiable. The 8.5 can't just know what they're doing — they must know what everyone else is doing. That's why some of the best hybrid midfielders are often seen pointing, talking, gesturing constantly. They're not just playing their role — they're coordinating others.

Interchangeability also creates a tactical dilemma for opponents. Man-mark the 8.5 and you risk being dragged out of shape. Let them roam and they'll exploit the pockets behind the press. It's a lose-lose scenario that elite teams engineer on purpose.

The modern 8.5 is like a Swiss Army knife — not because they do everything, but because they can become what the team needs, when it needs it.

Let's drill down into a few real-world examples to bring this to life.

Watch Ilkay Gündoğan under Pep Guardiola. One moment he's forming a double pivot alongside Rodri during the build-up, the next he's breaking the last line to finish like a striker. He adapts his role in real-time based on the movement of others — a full-back inverting, a winger coming inside, a centre-back stepping into midfield. It's football as a living organism, with the 8.5 as the neural connector.

Look at Martin Ødegaard at Arsenal. He's nominally the right-sided No. 8, but in reality, he's a shape-shifter. He drifts wide to combine with Saka and Timber/White, tucks in as a second playmaker behind the striker, and even drops next to the pivot when the press requires a third man deep. His flexibility unlocks Arsenal's positional play — not because he's everywhere, but because he knows exactly when to be somewhere.

Even someone like Jude Bellingham, who has exploded as a pseudo-attacking midfielder at Real Madrid, shows this tactical intelligence. He doesn't just score goals — he senses when to switch roles mid-phase. When to drop, when to break, when to hold. That awareness, that in-game IQ, is what makes him so lethal.

And it's not just in possession. Role-switching applies defensively too. The 8.5 might step into the front line to initiate a press, then drop to cover a vacated full-back zone when the shape is stretched. They switch gears constantly, and that duality is what keeps teams tactically resilient.

Coaches look for this adaptability when building their systems. They don't want rigid role-players. They want adaptable brains. The 8.5 is often the first name on the team sheet not because they're the flashiest, but because they make the system work.

You can teach passing drills. You can train pressing patterns. But you can't fake tactical intelligence. It's developed through reps, film work, and most importantly — autonomy. The best 8.5s are given freedom, but they earn it through consistent, intelligent decisions over 90 minutes. Not just what they do with the ball, but how they read the game without it.

They don't just play in the system. They *are* the system. And when they move, everything else moves with them.

The 8.5 as a System Optimiser

Modern football is a game of marginal gains. The difference between a Champions League-winning side and a team that crashes out in the group stage often lies in how well the system hums—not just the individual parts, but how they move together. Enter the 8.5: a midfielder whose fingerprints may not always show up on the stat sheet, but whose influence is everywhere. You don't build a great team around an 8.5; the 8.5 makes your team great.

This isn't about flashy stepovers or Hollywood passes. It's about a role that refines the system, smooths the edges, and turns tactical theory into fluid reality. Think of the 8.5 as your team's internal API—quietly running integrations between different parts of the pitch, allowing modules to talk to each other, and reducing system friction. Let's break down how this role elevates the collective.

Enhancing Possession and Counter-Pressing

Possession football—when done well—isn't about hoarding the ball. It's about control. And that control doesn't come from the backline stringing together 100 sideways passes. It comes from the players who can operate in chaos, under pressure, in between the lines. The 8.5 is your chaos conductor.

When you have a player who can receive on the half-turn in traffic, evade a press with a subtle drop of the shoulder, and immediately shift the game's axis—you're not just maintaining possession, you're weaponising it. This is where the 8.5 shines.

But the magic isn't only in what happens with the ball. It's in what happens the moment possession is lost. The best sides in the world don't defend by retreating. They defend by swarming. Counter-pressing isn't just a defensive tactic—it's an attacking one. And the 8.5 is often the first trigger.

You'll see it in teams like Liverpool under Klopp/Slot or Guardiola's Manchester City. The second the ball is turned over, the 8.5 is already closing down the nearest passing option, angling their run to cut off the switch, forcing play back into the trap. They don't just press—they anticipate where the next three passes might go.

It's this dual-role function—safe under pressure in possession, aggressive and intelligent out of possession—that allows the 8.5 to become the system's heartbeat. They're not just surviving the pressure. They're thriving in it, turning defence into platform, and platform into progression.

Supporting Wide and Central Overloads

In a world of compact low blocks and hyper-coached pressing systems, creating overloads has become the holy grail. Over-loads aren't just numerical advantages—they're psychological ones. When you can force the opposition to shift, to react, to overcompensate, you create space elsewhere. The 8.5 is the player who manipulates this dynamic.

Let's start centrally. Against teams that defend in a 4-4-2 or 4-5-1 block, your midfield is often matched man-for-man. The 8.5 disrupts that balance by drifting into pockets between the lines. Not quite a 10, not just an 8. They exist in the cracks.

Their movement forces decisions: does the holding mid-fielder step up and leave space behind? Does a centre-back break shape? Or does the 8.5 receive and turn with zero resistance? These micro-movements drag defenders out of structure. And once one piece steps out, the rest follows—not always willingly.

Now shift to the wide areas. Modern full-backs are no longer just defenders; they're auxiliary playmakers. When they invert into midfield or push high, the 8.5 adapts. They slide over to form triangles with the winger and full-back, creating 3v2s or 2v1s depending on the opposition's shape.

You'll often see them ghost into the half-space—one touch, spin, and release the overlapping runner. Or they'll hold their position just long enough to draw a defender out, then play the simple ball that unlocks the overload.

It's not about being the star in the move. It's about being the catalyst. The 8.5 makes your wide play more dangerous, not by being dominant in those zones, but by being present in a way that forces the opposition to make choices they don't want to make.

Enabling Tactical Transitions

Football matches are rarely won in static phases. They're won in the transitions—in that split second when a team shifts from attack to defence or vice versa. And this is where the 8.5 becomes invaluable. You're not just looking for a player who understands structure. You want one who can live in the unstructured.

When a team wins the ball high up the pitch, the 8.5 is often the first link. They're not making a Hollywood pass. They're scanning before the turnover, already identifying the weak side, the one-v-one on the far flank, or the blindside run behind the full-back.

They don't kill momentum with an extra touch. They accelerate it. One touch to secure, second touch to progress, third to release. That's the rhythm. If your 8.5 takes four or five touches, the transition is already dead. The defence is set. The opportunity is gone.

Now flip it. When you lose the ball, the 8.5's job isn't just to press. It's to stabilise. To fill the gaps left by overlapping full-backs. To delay the counter long enough for the rest of the team to reset. They're not launching into tackles—they're intercepting lanes, angling bodies, dictating where the ball has to go.

This dual-phase intelligence is what separates a good midfielder from a hybrid 8.5. They don't just play the game—they read the game's tempo, its rhythm, its momentum shifts. And they act accordingly. You can't teach this with a whiteboard.

You need players who can feel it.

But tactical transitions aren't just reactive. The best 8.5s initiate them. You'll see it in how they manage the tempo. When to slow the game down with a sideways pass and a subtle deceleration. When to inject pace with a disguised one-two and a burst into the box. It's this internal metronome that makes the role so valuable.

The 8.5 isn't just a connector. They're a disruptor. They make your system harder to read, harder to pin down, and harder to press. They live in the in-between moments—the milliseconds where most players hesitate and the best players act.

And for coaches, analysts, and players looking to elevate their tactical edge, this role is your cheat code. It won't show up in a traditional heat map or a basic stat package. But when you watch the game through the 8.5 lens, you'll start to see patterns you never saw before.

You'll see the player who starts the move three passes before the assist. The one who sprints 20 yards to close a passing lane no one else noticed. The one who floats into a zone, receives under pressure, and flips the direction of the attack with a disguised pass into space.

That's the system optimiser. Not the headline-maker, but the reason the headlines exist.

3

Decoding the 8.5 Toolkit: Skills That Matter

Technical Proficiencies

First-Touch and Scanning

You've heard the phrase *"the game is played before the ball arrives."* That's not a metaphor—it's a tactical reality. A hybrid 8.5, the player who operates between lines and manipulates space like a chess grandmaster, lives or dies by their first touch and pre-contact awareness. These aren't just technical competencies; they're neurological responses, shaped by habit, repetition, and hours of game-context training.

Let's break this down. The first touch isn't just about controlling the ball—it's about positioning it in your next movement's direction. A clean trap that sets the ball up to be played forward is a small win that cascades into larger tactical advantages. A bad first touch doesn't just lose the ball; it disrupts the rhythm of the entire team, especially in the central third where margins are tight and pressure is constant.

But the real magic happens before the ball even arrives. Scanning is the precursor to a meaningful first touch. The 8.5 needs to scan not once, but multiple times—before the pass, during the pass, and even as the ball is arriving. Why? Because the 8.5 often receives in crowded zones: between a collapsing double pivot, an aggressive centre-back stepping in, and a winger collapsing centrally. That scanning must reveal threats and opportunities—where's the press coming from, and where's the space to exploit?

This is where training environments often fall short. Too many drills are sterile. Static mannequins, pre-scripted patterns... they don't replicate the chaos of real play. The elite 8.5 trains in dynamic chaos—rondo variants with directional objectives, tight-space games, and live defenders who change pressing cues each repetition. The goal isn't just control under pressure—it's progression under pressure.

And here's the kicker: the very best 8.5s don't just scan to receive—they scan to deceive. They look left, take a touch right. They manipulate not just space, but the expectations of their opponents. That's a level of technical nuance that turns a good midfielder into a system-breaker.

Short and Medium-Range Passing Under Pressure

There's a difference between safety and security in midfield passing. Safety is a five-yard pass back to the centre-back. Security is threading a 12-yard vertical pass through the lines that breaks pressure and launches an attack. The 8.5 lives in this tension—risk versus reward, tempo versus control.

The modern game demands midfielders who can play in tight corridors with both feet. Coaches no longer ask, *"Can he pass?"* They ask, *"Can he pass under pressure, with the wrong foot, when three bodies are closing in?"* That's the standard. And for the 8.5, that's the baseline.

Short- and medium-range passing isn't about distance—it's about intention. *Is the pass to circulate or to provoke? Is it designed to bait the press or bypass it?* The 8.5 often operates as the relay runner between the deep pivot and the attacking midfielders. That means they're rarely passing in isolation. They're part of a chain. Every pass sets up the next action—whether it's a third-man run, a bounce-back combination, or a switch of play.

Under pressure, body shape is everything. The angle of the hips, the openness of the stance, the ability to disguise a pass with the eyes or body language—these are the *"non-stat"* skills that separate Tier 1 from Tier 2. You won't see them on a data dashboard, but analysts know when they're missing.

Elite-level 8.5s like Kevin De Bruyne or Jude Bellingham don't just play passes—they play narratives. They know when to speed the game up and when to slow it. They send messages to teammates through weight and direction: *"turn with this one," "lay it off," "move wide."* Passing becomes a language, and the 8.5 is fluent in it.

Progressive Ball-Carrying

If passing is the language of midfield, then ball-carrying is its accent. Every great 8.5 adds their own tone to it—some glide, some drive, some juke defenders out of their boots with a shimmy and half-touch. Regardless of style, progressive carrying is a core trait. You don't just need to move the ball—you need to move the game forward.

What makes progressive carrying so potent in the 8.5 role is its unpredictability. Defenders are trained to anticipate passes in positional play. But when the 8.5 picks up the ball in the half-space, turns, and drives directly at the back line, defensive shapes start to bend. A centre-back steps out, a full-back tucks in, and suddenly a winger is free on the far side. One carry can fracture an entire structure.

But it's not just about speed. It's about timing. Carry too early and you run into traffic. Carry too late and the window closes. The best 8.5s understand tempo—not just theirs, but the game's. They choose moments when the opposition shape is most vulnerable: after a lost duel, during a delayed press, or when a midfielder is caught ball-watching.

Footwork matters. It's not flashy tricks—it's efficient move-ment. A drop of the shoulder to shift a defender's weight, a quick outside-in touch to break a line, a sudden deceleration to draw a foul and reset the rhythm. These micro-movements aren't stylistic—they're strategic.

And let's talk about the psychological effect. When a mid-fielder carries with purpose, he sends a message to both teams: *"We're not waiting for the game to come to us—we're taking it."* That assertiveness can flip a passive phase into an aggressive one. It changes the posture of the team. You start seeing full-backs pushing on, wingers making inverted runs, and centre-forwards checking deeper to receive. One carry. That's all it takes.

Progressive ball-carrying also opens up the concept of "*carry-to-draw.*" This is where the 8.5 intentionally drives into contact—not to beat the man, but to force a reaction. Once the defender steps, the ball is released into the now-vacated zone. Think of it as a tactical bait. It's not about beating the man—it's about weaponising attention.

The Two-Footed Imperative

Let's cut through the fluff: if you're playing in central areas at a high level and you can't pass, receive, or carry with both feet, you're a liability. The 8.5 operates in 360-degree zones. Pressures come from behind, from the blindside, from angles that punish predictable players.

Being two-footed isn't just about ambidexterity—it's about optionality. The more directions you can turn, the more angles you can play, the harder you are to press. It's geometry meets psychology. Force a one-footed midfielder onto their weak side, and you've already won half the battle. But force a two-footed 8.5, and they'll just adapt.

Training this isn't about isolated reps. It's about constraints. Small-sided games where you can only play with your weak foot. Rondos where you must receive on one foot and release with the other. Drills where passing lanes are blocked unless you open up via the weaker side. Train in discomfort until it becomes your default.

The best two-footed players aren't symmetrical—they're unpredictable. Their left foot doesn't mirror the right; it complements it. Think of Kevin De Bruyne whipping crosses with either foot, or Luka Modrić playing disguised passes into tight spaces from either side. That's the standard. And for the 8.5, that's the expectation.

Tactical Intelligence

There's a difference between knowing a thing and being able to do it at speed, under pressure, in a stadium vibrating with tension. The modern 8.5—the hybrid midfielder who's neither a pure 8 nor a traditional 10—lives in that gap between theory and application. You can teach a player to pass, trap, dribble. But teaching them how to *think*? That's where roles evolve and systems transform.

This is where tactical intelligence becomes the real separator. Not just awareness, but the kind of situational cognition that lets a player read the game two passes ahead. Not just positioning, but the ability to *manipulate* space. The 8.5 doesn't wait for the game to happen—they shape it.

Let's break down three of the most essential cognitive weapons in the 8.5's arsenal.

Timing of Third-Man Runs

If you're only watching the player on the ball, you've already missed the plot. The real artistry often happens off-camera: the third-man run. It's not about beating a man with the ball. It's about moving in a way that lets your teammate beat two lines *without* the ball.

Here's what separates the top-tier 8.5s: they don't just run into space. They *create* it. They delay. They accelerate. They ghost into zones that defenders didn't know needed protecting.

Take Kevin De Bruyne. He doesn't demand the ball in tight areas. He drifts wide, lets the 10 receive centrally, then times his burst into the half-space *after* the centre-back has stepped.

33

That's not intuition—it's pattern recognition honed over thousands of reps. He knows the second man's movement triggers the third man's reward.

For you as a coach, analyst, or player, here's the thing: third-man runs are not freelance moves. They are system-connected actions. They depend on trust, timing, and clarity. You can't run if the first man doesn't check in. You can't receive if the second man doesn't play with the correct tempo.

Drills alone won't breed this instinct. You need scenario-based training, where players learn to read triggers: body shape of the passer, positioning of the defenders, the angle of the receiver's run. The 8.5 has to see all of it in real time—and most importantly, act *before* the space opens.

Now, zoom out. In matches where the tempo is high and pressing is relentless, the 8.5's capacity to time these runs becomes the difference between recycling the ball and slicing open the opposition. It's not about how often they run. It's about *when* they do it.

Occupying Half-Spaces

The pitch isn't divided into neat thirds when you're operating between the lines. It's a chessboard, and the half-spaces are where the bishops live—diagonal, dynamic, and devastating when used well.

The half-space lies between the central channel and the wing, vertically aligned with the edge of the penalty area. Too wide for a centre-back, too narrow for a full-back, and often ignored by a traditional pivot. This is the 8.5's playground.

Here's the nuance: it's not just about standing there. It's

34

about *arriving* there at the right moment. Static positioning in the half-space invites pressure. But dynamic movement— looping runs, inside-to-outside drifts, delayed arrivals—create confusion. Defenders hate grey areas, and the half-space is a fog of war.

Think of Thomas Müller, the original Raumdeuter. He doesn't dazzle with flair, but his timing and positioning in the half-spaces destabilise entire back lines. He drags defenders out. He opens passing lanes for others. And he creates second balls in dangerous zones.

Now reverse-engineer that to the training ground. What does occupying the half-space *look like* in a possession drill? It's not just staying wide or central—it's knowing when to drift to receive, when to stretch vertically, and when to vacate to allow an underlapping full-back to fill the zone.

For the 8.5, this zone becomes a launchpad.

From the half-space, you can:

· Play vertical passes into the striker's feet.
· Combine with overlapping full-backs.
· Switch the play with a diagonal ball across the pitch.
· Attack the far post on a late run.

The key is dual-threat positioning. You want to be close enough to combine with central players, but far enough to isolate a wide defender. It's a balancing act—too central, and you clog the pivot's space; too wide, and you lose your connection to the buildup.

This is why players like Martin Ødegaard thrive in these roles. He doesn't just receive in the half-space—he *manages* it. He knows when to drop to support the build, when to push high to pin the back line, and when to vacate to let the winger operate 1v1.

As a coach or analyst, it's not enough to say *"occupy the half-space."* You need to define *why*, *when*, and *how*. Is it to attract a marker and free the pivot? Is it to overload the wing? Is it to create a triangle with the striker and wide player? Each use case has a different behavioural cue.

Recognising Pressing Triggers

This one separates the thinkers from the reactors. Pressing triggers are the moments when the opposition decides to apply pressure. The 8.5 must know these *better* than the opposition. It's not just about avoiding the press—it's about weaponising it.

Recognising pressing triggers means seeing the trap *before* it's set.

There are standard triggers: a back pass, a poor touch, a sideways ball to a full-back near the line. But elite midfielders go deeper. They recognise *body shape* as a trigger. If a centre-back receives side-on, with the wrong foot forward, the press is coming. If the pivot drops into the back line and no one fills the vacated space, pressing ensues.

The 8.5's job in these moments? Offer solutions. *Fast.*

You have to become the release valve. If your centre-back is about to be pressed, you need to check into a space that opens a passing lane. If the pivot is trapped, you must rotate into their role without hesitation. If the winger is about to be boxed in, you'd better be near enough to give them an outlet.

But it's not just about availability. It's about *inviting* the press in a way that creates chaos—then exploiting it. Think of Frenkie de Jong at Barcelona, and particularly in his Ajax days. He'd drop deep, bait two midfielders, then slalom into space after a quick wall pass. That's not luck. That's awareness fused with nerve.

In tactical periodisation training, you need to simulate these moments. Not just rondos, but real, match-tempo scenarios where players are forced to read pressure patterns and *act in anticipation*, not reaction.

For analysts, this is gold. Track how often your 8.5 offers themselves as a press-resistant outlet. Count how many times they rotate into the pivot line when a full-back is isolated. Measure their recovery runs *after* a pressing trigger fails— because the game doesn't stop when the trap is broken. The 8.5 must sprint back into zone 14, ready to snuff out the counter.

At the elite level, this becomes psychological warfare. The 8.5 who sees the press coming not only survives it—they set the tempo for the next phase. They make the opposition doubt the value of pressing at all.

To be that player, you need more than lungs and legs. You need pattern recognition, tactical empathy, and a sixth sense for danger. The kind of intelligence that sees the dominoes falling *before* the first one is touched.

Tactical intelligence isn't about memorising diagrams or reciting formations. It's about decision-making in the blur. The 8.5 exists in that blur—not on the whiteboard, but in the gaps between roles, the seams between lines, and the seconds between chaos and clarity.

You don't train intelligence like you train stamina. You develop it through high-context reps, guided reflection, and exposure to complexity. And once a player has it, systems bend to their will. Not the other way around.

Physical and Psychological Attributes

There's a reason the true 8.5s stand out—not just on the ball, but in how they move, recover, read space, and carry themselves when the game turns chaotic. This role isn't for the faint-hearted. It's for the player who can sprint in the 90th as if it's the 10th, who stays calm when the pitch is burning, and who makes the right call when everyone else is guessing. If you're going to thrive as a hybrid midfielder, your toolbox can't just be technical or tactical. You need a body that doesn't break and a mind that doesn't blink.

Stamina and Spatial Awareness

Let's start with the lungs. If you're not covering ground, you're not an 8.5. You're a 10 that forgot to drop back. Or an 8 that forgot to step forward. The hybrid midfielder is the definition of relentless. Think of it this way: if a GPS tracker isn't showing your name in the top three for high-intensity distance covered, you're not doing enough.

But it's not just about running. It's about where you're running—and when.

The best 8.5s don't chase the ball like dogs after a frisbee. They move like chess players think: two, three, four passes ahead. They understand that space isn't just where the ball is; it's where the ball wants to go next.

Look at Kevin De Bruyne when City build up. He doesn't sprint aimlessly. He jogs into half-spaces, slows to a walk, then bursts into a gap as if reacting to a sixth sense. That's not luck. That's spatial awareness fused with elite stamina—because he knows the burst only matters if he can do it again, and again, and again.

Training this isn't just about running laps. It's small-sided games with compressed space and time. It's working with GPS data to understand your heatmaps. It's sprint-repeat drills with decision-making baked in—because the 8.5 doesn't need to just move. They need to move with purpose, every time.

And the beauty? Once you develop this engine, it becomes your tactical weapon. You become the player that turns a 4-3-3 into a 2-3-5 in possession and a 4-5-1 out of it—without the manager needing to change the shape.

Mental Resilience in Transitions

The 8.5 exists in the game's most volatile zone: between structure and chaos. Transitions—those wild, unpredictable, uncoached phases where formations break and instincts take over—are their natural habitat.

When a counter starts, most players panic. They either sprint back blindly or freeze. The 8.5? They process, prioritise, and act. They know whether the ball needs to be stopped at source or delayed. They know when to foul, when to press, when to recover space. And that decision has to happen in a second— while their heart rate is at 180 bpm.

Mental resilience here isn't something you can teach in a classroom. It's forged in match scenarios, in failure, in repetition. Managers like Jaissle and Nagelsmann stress these phases in training with chaotic drills: two-ball transitions, uneven numbers, time-constrained recoveries. They're not just building fitness. They're stress-testing your mind.

Think of N'Golo Kanté in the 2018 World Cup. Every transition went through him. He didn't just run. He read. He anticipated. And more importantly, he never switched off. That's mental resilience. That's what separates the elite 8.5s from the rest.

There's also a psychological layer here that coaches often miss: emotional control. Transitions are emotionally loaded. A lost ball. A missed tackle. A chance gone begging. The 8.5 needs to park that emotion instantly. Flipping between attack and defence isn't just about legs—it's about mindset. You can't dwell. You can't whine. You reset and go.

And if you're coaching this role, that's your job too. Build drills that punish emotional lag. Run sessions where bad decisions have instant consequences. Not to embarrass—but to simulate pressure. Because matchday won't wait for your midfielder to get their head right.

Decision-Making Under Duress

If there's a single trait that defines the hybrid midfielder, it's this: they consistently make the right choice when everything around them is wrong. Wrong angles. Wrong spacing. Wrong passes. The game is messy, but they're not. They stay clean.

Decision-making under pressure is often misunderstood. It's not about always choosing the safest pass. It's about knowing what the situation demands. Sometimes that's a disguised ball through the lines. Sometimes it's a back-pass to reset. Sometimes it's a foul.

The 8.5 sees the options—then acts with conviction.

Let's go deeper. There are three types of pressure every hybrid midfielder faces:

1. **Time Pressure** – A defender closing fast. You've got milliseconds to control, scan, and release.
2. **Tactical Pressure** – You're in the middle of a trap. The opposition is funnelling you into a zone.
3. **Emotional Pressure** – The crowd's roaring. Your team is chasing a goal. You just lost the ball.

The elite 8.5s handle all three in stride. Why? Because they're trained for it. Their routines are built on repetition and clarity. They trust their triggers.

Look at Ilkay Gündoğan. He doesn't just play passes; he plays percentages. Every time he receives, he's already mapped three exits. That's not improvisation—it's programming.

You build this in training by designing drills that compress time and space. Use opponents instead of mannequins. Mix in overloads. Add reactive cues. And crucially, film everything. Because the 8.5 needs to watch themselves under pressure to understand their patterns.

But there's also a neurological component here. Studies in elite sport show that decision quality under stress is linked to heart rate variability and cognitive load. In simple terms: if your brain's overstimulated, your choices suck.

So, recovery matters. Sleep matters. Breathing techniques matter. Some clubs are now integrating mindfulness training and HRV monitoring into midfielder development—not as a gimmick, but as a performance edge.

And here's the twist: the best 8.5s don't just survive under pressure. They thrive in it. They use pressure to manipulate.

41

They bait defenders. They disguise intentions. They create chaos, then step into the calm.

That's the final layer. Not just decision-making under duress—but using duress as a weapon.

You want your 8.5 to do more than escape pressure. You want them to shape it.

Watch how Martin Ødegaard drops his shoulder under pressure, not to evade—but to draw in a second marker and release a teammate. That's not just flair. That's a calculated decision, made in a high-stakes moment, with full awareness of the tactical chain reaction.

This is what makes the hybrid midfielder indispensable. They're not just technical or tactical. They're physiological and psychological anomalies. They're the ones who press, recover, create, and control—all while looking like they've got time.

You don't find them. You build them. You stress them. And if they survive, you unleash them.

Half-Time Talk: Your 60-Second Assist

Let's pause for a moment.

You've made it through the first three chapters. That means you're one of us — a student of the modern game, obsessed with the details that others miss. You see the pitch differently now. The role of the 8.5 isn't just a concept anymore — it's a lens. A tactical superpower. A shift in your footballing vocabulary.

Here's the pass I'm sending your way:

If this book has sparked something in you — an insight, a new idea, a tactical connection — would you take 60 seconds to leave a quick review?

Think of it this way:

There's a young coach in Lisbon. A youth player in Chicago. A data analyst in Tokyo. Each one searching for clarity in the chaos of modern football. Your review is the through ball that helps them find this book — and maybe, their next breakthrough.

Here's how to assist in three simple steps:

1. If you're reading on Kindle:
2. Scroll to the very end of the book.
3. A prompt to leave a review will pop up like a well-timed overlap. Tap it.
4. Drop your honest thoughts — one sentence, ten sentences, whatever feels right.
5. If you're listening on Audible:
6. Tap the three dots in the upper right corner of your screen.
7. Select "Rate & Review."
8. Let others know what value you've found in these pages.
9. If you're on Amazon:
10. Search for The Hybrid 8.5 on the Amazon store.
11. Scroll down to "Customer Reviews."
12. Click "Write a customer review." That's your moment to shine.

This book isn't backed by a publisher's marketing machine. It spreads the same way great tactical ideas do — word of mouth, passionate communities, and one person sharing insight with another.

If you've gained value here, pay it forward. Leave a review and help someone else unlock the role of the 8.5 — and maybe even transform the way they read the game.

Thanks for being part of this journey.

Now, let's get back out there. Second half's starting.

4

The Evolution of Systems: How Formations Created the 8.5

From 4-4-2 to 4-3-3

There's a reason the 4-4-2 is often spoken about in nostal-gic tones—it was once the blueprint for balance. Symmetry. Simplicity. And for a long time, it worked. Two central mid-fielders, one holding, one box-to-box. Wingers who hugged the touchline. Two strikers hunting in tandem. It was the shape of title-winning sides, World Cup champions, and grassroots Sunday league teams alike. But as the game evolved—faster, tighter, more spatially intelligent—it became clear: the 4-4-2 was no longer enough.

You don't build a hybrid midfielder in a vacuum. Tactical systems shape roles, define responsibilities, and create the conditions for emergence. The 8.5 didn't just appear—it was engineered, intentionally or not, by the systems that demanded more from midfielders.

Let's pull the curtain back on how the shift from 4-4-2 to

4-3-3 quietly rewired the architecture of midfield, opening the door for the hybrid role to be born.

Structural Limitations of Classic Shapes

The 4-4-2 was designed for clarity. Two banks of four, zonal discipline, and vertical link-up between midfield and attack. But clarity comes at a cost: rigidity.

In a 4-4-2, central midfielders are stretched—defensively responsible and expected to support forward transitions. But they're often outnumbered. Against a 4-3-3 or a 4-2-3-1, those two central players are outflanked and outmanoeuvred. You might win the second ball, but you rarely control the rhythm.

And control is everything in modern football.

What made the 4-4-2 vulnerable wasn't just numerical disadvantage—it was spatial exposure. The half-spaces, those narrow vertical corridors between the centre and the wing, were left unguarded. Opponents began exploiting these grey zones, operating in pockets where 4-4-2 midfielders couldn't reach without abandoning their zones.

Enter the need for a third midfielder. Not just a destroyer. Not just a passer. But someone who could operate in those half-spaces, connect phases, and serve as a pivot for tactical flexibility.

The Rise of the Single Pivot

When teams shifted to the 4-3-3, they didn't just add a midfielder—they redefined the midfield hierarchy. The single pivot became the metronome. Think Sergio Busquets at Barcelona, Michael Carrick at Manchester United, or Xabi Alonso during his Liverpool and Real Madrid days. These weren't flashy players. They weren't necessarily racking up goals or assists. But they dictated tempo, dropped between centre-backs to form a temporary back three, and initiated build-up with surgical precision.

This freed the two advanced midfielders to do something revolutionary: play between the lines.

No longer shackled by the need to hold position, these midfielders could drift. One could push high, the other drop slightly deeper. One could slide wide to create overloads with the winger, the other could ghost into the box. The midfield triangle became asymmetrical—fluid, dynamic, and unpredictable.

This asymmetry is the birthplace of the 8.5.

You had one player who wasn't quite a No. 8 in the traditional sense—ball-winner, shuttler, engine. Nor was he a classic No. 10—luxury creator, free of defensive duty. He was both. And neither. He was the in-between: a role built on adaptability, spatial awareness, and multi-phase influence.

Shift Towards Midfield Dynamism

There's a phrase used by elite coaches that you'll hear whispered in tactical sessions: *"Control the midfield, control the game."* But controlling the midfield in the modern game isn't just about *numbers*—it's about *layers*.

The evolution from flat to staggered midfield lines was more than cosmetic. It introduced verticality—players occupying different horizontal planes. This layering made pressing harder for opponents. It opened new passing lanes. And it forced midfielders to think in three dimensions, not two.

In a 4-3-3, the interior midfielders (often called *"free 8s"*) are expected to contribute to both attacking and defensive phases. But within that expectation emerged a divergence. One interior midfielder began to play closer to the forward line—pressing high, arriving late in the box, linking with the striker. The other played slightly deeper—recycling possession, offering defensive cover, and plugging gaps.

But in truly progressive systems, that division wasn't static. The players rotated. Interchanged. Adapted based on the opponent's press, the game state, and positional triggers. The interior midfielder became a shape-shifter.

This is where the 8.5 comes alive: not defined by fixed positioning, but by functional adaptability.

You see it in Ilkay Gündoğan under Pep Guardiola. One moment, he's part of the midfield build-up; the next, he's arriving unmarked at the edge of the six-yard box. You see it in Bernardo Silva—pressing like a terrier, drifting into the half-space, then tucking in as an auxiliary full-back to retain possession.

These aren't traditional roles. They're emergent behaviours

48

shaped by system demands.

And it's not just at the elite level. The ripple effect of 4-3-3's dominance has filtered into youth academies, amateur coaching sessions, and national team setups. Young midfielders are no longer taught to play as a "6" or a "10" exclusively. They're taught to understand space, interpret movement, and shift roles dynamically based on the moment. They're taught to be hybrids.

Why This Shift Matters to You

If you're a coach, this evolution should challenge how you think about roles. Are you boxing players into static positions because the formation dictates it? Or are you building systems that allow role fluidity based on player intelligence?

If you're a player, especially a midfielder, understand this: your value skyrockets when you can interpret space and switch roles within a single phase. Being technically gifted is great. But being tactically fluent is transformative.

And if you're an analyst or a scout, stop looking for players who only fit into traditional buckets. Start identifying those who do multiple things well—those who connect build-up, support wide overloads, and arrive late in the final third. Those who can be the 8.5, even if they're not labelled as such.

Formations aren't relics—they're frameworks. But the best systems don't constrain players. They empower them. The shift from 4-4-2 to 4-3-3 didn't just change where players stood on the pitch. It changed how they thought, how they moved, how they affected the game.

The 8.5 was born from this shift—not as a tactical invention, but as a necessity. A response to the growing demand for players who could do more, think quicker, and adapt faster.

You don't train a hybrid role. You cultivate it through systems that demand decision-making, not just execution.

The 4-3-3 made that possible. And in doing so, it cracked open the door to a new kind of midfielder—one who doesn't just fit into a system but enhances it.

The 4-2-3-1 and the Rise of the Playmaker

There's a reason the 4-2-3-1 became the default setting for a generation of coaches. It offered the best of multiple tactical worlds—defensive stability with a double pivot, attacking thrust through a central playmaker, and width from advanced wingers. But more than that, it created a platform that allowed the modern 8.5 to evolve in the shadows of the number 10. The 4-2-3-1 didn't just accommodate creativity—it demanded it. And in doing so, it redefined the architecture of the midfield.

Central Overloads and Dual Pivots

The emergence of the 4-2-3-1 was no accident. It was a response. A counter to the vulnerabilities of the flat 4-4-2 and an answer to the pressing demands of the modern game. Coaches needed more control in midfield, and the dual pivot offered just that.

When you deploy two holding midfielders—typically a mix of a destroyer and a distributor—you create a platform. Think Xabi Alonso and Sami Khedira. Sergio Busquets and Xavi (before the latter was pushed higher). The idea was simple: secure the base, dominate the middle, and let the attacking midfield trio go to work.

But here's the nuance that tactical observers live for. The '2' in the 4-2-3-1 wasn't always a static block. One would often sit, the other shuttle. And this is where the seeds of the 8.5 were sown. Because between those pivots and the number 10 sat a vacuum—a space often unoccupied, but brimming with potential. Midfielders who could ghost between these lines started to thrive. They weren't strictly attacking mids, nor were they conventional box-to-box players. They were part-architect, part-infiltrator.

This central overload became a key feature. With a double pivot securing possession and recycling play, teams could afford to push the '3' line higher. The result? Space manipulation. Overloads in the middle third that forced opponents to collapse centrally, creating room out wide for full-backs and inverted wingers to exploit. Or, if the press was committed wide, the 8.5 could exploit half-spaces with delayed runs and third-man combinations.

In essence, the dual pivot didn't just protect—it enabled. It allowed one of the trio ahead to drop in, receive under pressure, and turn. Or to make those clever shuttle runs between the lines, disguised as decoys but designed to fracture defensive shape. The hybrid midfielder found a habitat here. Not as the focal point like the 10, and not shackled like the deeper pivots. But as the connector. The interpreter.

Role of the Advanced Midfielder

The number 10 in the 4-2-3-1 was once a sacred role.

Zidane. Riquelme. Kaká. They were the artists. Given freedom between the lines, they floated. They dictated. But as pressing intensity increased and the spaces between lines diminished, the luxury of a free-roaming playmaker became harder to accommodate.

This is where the savvy coaches began to tweak. That central '3' line was no longer a free pass for artistry. It became a zone of responsibility. Players in the 10 position now had to press, track, and counter-press. The profile of the advanced midfielder started to shift—from the luxury creator to the industrious hybrid.

Enter the 8.5.

Not every team was blessed with a classic 10. Some didn't want one. In response, managers began installing players more accustomed to the number 8 role into this space. They had the lungs, the legs, and the brain to operate in tight areas. They could press like midfielders and create like attackers. early Dele Alli, early Kai Havertz, Thomas Müller—players often misunderstood because they didn't fit the historical moulds. They weren't classic 10s. They weren't eights. They were something in between. In the 4-2-3-1, this role evolved. The '10' wasn't a singular identity anymore.

Coaches began to deploy players who could start as a midfielder and finish moves like a striker. They had the timing to arrive late in the box, the intuition to press passing lanes, and the spatial literacy to rotate with wingers or central midfielders. These were players who understood both attacking and transitional phases in equal measure.

Some teams even began to invert the triangle in possession. Shifting from a 4-2-3-1 into a 4-3-3 shape when building up—allowing the central attacking midfielder to drop into a deeper pocket, and one of the pivots to push higher. The lines blurred. The 8.5 quietly emerged—not as a fixed role, but as a dynamic function dependent on the team's rhythm.

The modernised advanced midfielder in the 4-2-3-1 wasn't just adding to the attack. They were often the first line of defence. And it's in that duality—the capacity to break lines and block them—that the 8.5 finds its tactical identity.

Tactical Implications for Pressing Systems

The 4-2-3-1 gave pressing a new face. With a three-man line behind the striker, coaches now had more flexibility to initiate pressure high up the pitch. And guess who often triggered that press? The central advanced midfielder.

Traditional number 10s weren't built for this. They didn't have the engine. But hybrid midfielders—those with the instincts of a creator and the appetite of a ball-winner—thrived. The pressing structure in a 4-2-3-1 often relied on the central player in the '3' line to block passing lanes to the opposition pivot, angle their body to force play wide, or jump onto centre-backs when the striker curved their run. This wasn't artistry—it was architecture.

The 8.5 became the tactical fulcrum of pressing systems. They were the ones who set the tone. If they stepped late, the whole press unravelled. If they timed it right, they could funnel opponents into traps—towards the sidelines or into zones where the pivot could pounce. This required intelligence, anticipation, and relentless scanning.

And the reward? Once possession was regained, they were already in prime territory—between the lines, facing goal. They didn't need to arrive; they were already there. In these moments, the hybrid midfielder became the chaos conductor. One touch to shift the angle, then a disguised ball into a forward. Or a quick give-and-go with a wide player. Or even a burst into the box themselves.

In pressing systems, the 8.5 wasn't just a cog. They were the ignition. Their positioning determined the angle of the trap. Their anticipation dictated the success of the transition. They weren't pressing for the sake of it—they were pressing with purpose. To create. To destabilise. To flip the game.

And this is where the 4-2-3-1 proved its versatility. It allowed for structural integrity with the double pivot, but also gave the 8.5 the freedom to hunt in packs. The shape could morph into a 4-4-2 out of possession, with the central attacking midfielder stepping up alongside the striker. Or it could shift into a narrow 4-3-3, depending on the trigger. The 8.5 had to understand these nuances—not just where to be, but when to be there.

Ultimately, the tactical implications of the 4-2-3-1 weren't limited to what happened on the ball. The pressing patterns, rotation triggers, and spatial manipulation off the ball all demanded midfielders who could think a phase ahead. The 8.5 didn't just survive in this formation—they flourished. Because it required a player who could do a bit of everything, all the time.

And in a game increasingly defined by transitions, there's no room for passengers. You either influence the game in multiple phases, or you get replaced. The 4-2-3-1 didn't just create space for the 8.5. It depended on them.

Modern Trends: 3-2-5s and Box Midfields

Inverted Full-Backs and Midfield Overloads

Let's get blunt: the era of the chalk-on-boots full-back is over. The idea that wide defenders should hug the touchline and whip in crosses like it's 2004? Obsolete for most elite setups. Inverted full-backs are the tactical evolution that flipped the game – literally and figuratively – and they've become one of the key enablers of the 8.5 role.

You've seen it. João Cancelo stepping into central midfield zones from full-back. Achraf Hakimi drifting inside to create a numerical advantage. This isn't just about freedom of movement – it's about deliberate central overloads. When a full-back inverts, they're not abandoning their flank; they're forming a midfield triangle or square that stretches and breaks pressing shapes. It's geometry as much as it is football.

The 3-2-5 build-up structure is where this all gets interesting. Picture three centre-backs forming the last line (often helped by a pivot who drops in), two central midfielders in front – and one or both full-backs becoming part of that two. What you get is a pseudo-double pivot that's actually more dynamic than static. And now you've got five players ahead, occupying the forward and half-space lines. This is where your 8.5 thrives.

The hybrid midfielder benefits from this shape because it creates fluidity in occupation. The inverted full-back pulls an opposing winger or midfielder inside, opening up lanes. That's your cue – the 8.5 steps into the gap, receives on the half-turn, and now the dominoes start falling. It's not just movement; it's magnetism in action. Everyone is drawn to the ball, and the 8.5 exploits what they leave behind.

This system also demands an almost telepathic relationship between the 8.5 and the inverted full-back. They'll often occupy the same zones in different phases. One sits, one goes. One receives, one screens. You're not just sharing space – you're co-authoring every passage of play.

And tactically, it gives you flexibility in pressing transitions. If possession is lost, the inverted full-back is already in the midfield zone to counter-press. The 8.5, too, is close to the action. Central compactness is preserved, and recovery routes are short. This isn't just stylistic – it's structural efficiency.

Old-school thinkers might see this as blasphemy. *"Full-backs should defend wide."* But the smart teams know better: central overloads win matches, and inverted roles enable that. The 8.5 is no longer working in isolation – they're part of a tightly coordinated interior network.

Creating Central Superiority

This is where the chessboard expands. In a 3-2-5 or a box midfield, the objective is brutal in its simplicity: own the centre. Not share, not compete – dominate. Every tactical system that matters today builds around this principle. And the 8.5 is your bishop – diagonally dangerous, always a move ahead.

Central superiority isn't just about numbers; it's about influence. You can have five players in the middle and still lose the battle if they're static or poorly positioned. The 8.5 isn't just a body in the zone – they're the one pulling strings. Think of them as the pressure-release valve and the ignition switch, simultaneously. It's a rare balance, and modern systems are designed to bring it out.

Coaches have started to weaponise the midfield in new ways. Instead of a flat three, you'll often see a staggered shape – one deeper pivot, two advanced 8s, or a 10 and an 8. In some systems, it morphs into a 2+2 square, the famous *"box midfield."* This shape is devastating when deployed correctly. It provides passing options at multiple angles and allows the 8.5 to ghost between the lines without a marker glued to them.

The beauty of the box is in its dynamism. One diagonal cut from the 8.5, and you've broken the opposition's midfield line. One touch around the corner, and you're behind the press. The 8.5 becomes the pivot point around which the attack revolves, often without even touching the ball. Their positioning alone manipulates defenders, dragging them out or freezing them in place.

Verticality is the name of the game. Teams are now obsessed with moving through the thirds quickly but intelligently. The 8.5 is central to this – not as a long-ball merchant, but as a space invader. They find the pockets just before they open, receive with orientation already set, and either release a runner or carry into the next zone.

And when you add in the inverted full-back or the inside-moving winger, you start seeing triangles form on demand. The 8.5 becomes the hinge between the deeper pivot and the attacking five. They're not just linking – they're dictating.

It's also where pressing traps are avoided. Many teams now bait the press in central areas just to exploit the space it vacates. The 8.5 has to be brave here – receiving under pressure, knowing exactly where their next touch goes. Mistime it and you're exposed. Nail it, and your team is on the break with numerical superiority.

You're not playing for possession anymore – you're playing

to stretch the opponent until they break their shape. That's what central superiority is about. Not control for control's sake, but control with purpose. And the 8.5 is your scalpel.

The 8.5 in Positionally Fluid Systems

Now we're in the deep end. Positionally fluid systems are the cutting edge of tactical evolution – where roles aren't fixed, zones are shared, and movement is the language of structure. If you're not building around fluidity in modern football, you're building to be beaten. The 8.5 doesn't just survive in these environments – they thrive.

In these systems, traditional positions dissolve. You'll see centre-backs stepping into midfield, wingers tucking into the half-space, and midfielders making runs beyond the striker. It's chaos on the surface, but underneath, it's all mapped out. The 8.5 is often the switchboard operator – receiving signals from every corner and distributing action accordingly.

One minute they're a high-pressing 10, the next they're a deep-lying 6. Then they're interchanging with the full-back, or sliding into the half-space to overload the flank. It's not about position anymore – it's about function. What does the team need in this phase? That's the question the 8.5 answers, almost subconsciously.

You've seen this expressed in teams like Manchester City or Brighton under De Zerbi – where roles are interchangeable, but responsibilities are clear. It takes enormous intelligence to operate in these systems. You can't just be technically sharp – you have to understand spacing, timing, and opponent psychology. The 8.5 becomes a shape-shifter. One moment a connector, the next a penetrator, then a stabiliser.

This demands a unique type of player. One who isn't just gifted on the ball, but who scans constantly, processes information rapidly, and acts with conviction. They don't need to be the flashiest – in fact, the best 8.5s often go unnoticed by casual fans. But for coaches and analysts? They're gold dust. Their movements set the rhythm. Their decisions shape the phase.

What makes this role so vital in fluid systems is its elasticity. The 8.5 stretches the opponent's midfield vertically and laterally. By occupying multiple vertical lanes – from deep central to advanced half-space – they disrupt marking schemes and create uncertainty. Who picks them up? A centre-back steps out and leaves space in behind. A midfielder tracks and gets dragged out of shape. It's a lose-lose for the opposition.

And when the ball is turned over, the 8.5 is often already in a position to either press or recover. That's the hidden genius of fluid systems – they're not just about attack. They're about being one pass away from defensive solidity. The 8.5 is the hinge. They're always connected to both ends of the pitch.

You can't coach this role through static drills. You develop it through scenario training, through teaching players to read patterns and react in real time. The 8.5 isn't a system-dependent luxury – they're the system's embodiment. Their presence allows positional rotations to occur without losing structure. They're the glue.

When you zoom out, you realise that the rise of the 8.5 isn't just about a new type of midfielder. It's about a new way of understanding football. Systems are no longer rigid blueprints – they're living organisms. And the 8.5 is the neural pathway that lets it all flow.

5

The 8.5 in Possession: Making the Invisible Visible

Progressing Play

Receiving Between Lines

If you want to understand modern football's chessboard, start with the 8.5 receiving the ball between the lines. This is where geometry meets bravery. It's not about standing in a pocket of space—it's about arriving in one, at the precise moment defenders commit forward or shift sideways. That split-second delay, that micro-adjustment of timing, is what separates a good midfielder from a systemic disruptor.

The 8.5 doesn't just receive the ball; they scan before the pass is even played. Think of it as pre-loading a decision. By the time the ball arrives, they already know where it's going next. This is scanning in its most advanced form—not just seeing, but predicting. It's the art of knowing where space is about to appear, not where it already exists.

Take Martin Ødegaard. Watch how he angles his body before receiving a vertical pass from a pivot. He positions himself half-turned, one shoulder pointed towards the opposition goal, the other towards the touchline. Why? This positioning opens up two passing lanes and a dribble route simultaneously. Defenders hesitate. A single touch and he's away, either playing a third-man combination or driving forward himself. He's not just a receiver—he's a directional compass for the entire attack.

The key is trust from teammates. The centre-backs and pivots must believe the 8.5 can take a risk and retain possession in traffic. Without that trust, you don't get progression. You get recycling. And recycling is just motion without intent.

Driving into Space

Once the ball is received between the lines, the next decision is whether to pass or carry. The 8.5 often chooses the latter—not out of ego, but because carrying draws defenders and fractures defensive blocks. It turns static lines into broken shapes. And broken shapes are where chances are born.

Carrying isn't about showboating with the ball glued to your foot. It's about timing your acceleration into the space just before it closes. You're not running into space—you're dragging defenders into it. The best 8.5s use their body like a shield and a weapon. They lean into contact, bait pressure, and then explode. Think of Frenkie de Jong gliding past two pressing midfielders, pulling the opposition's shape out of sync. It's chaos, but it's calculated.

The 8.5 doesn't need to beat a man every time. Sometimes it's about committing one defender, forcing the back line to contract, and then slipping a pass into the newly vacated channel. This is progression with purpose. You're not carrying for yards—you're carrying for disorganisation.

And this is where your conditioning comes in. These repeated accelerations—10 to 15 metres at a time—don't always show up in highlight reels. But they're the heartbeat of your side's forward momentum. Without them, possession becomes sterile. With them, it becomes surgical.

Disrupting Defensive Blocks

Modern defences are zonal, compact, and ruthlessly drilled. A good block can suffocate even the most technically slick side. That's why the 8.5 is so crucial—they're the disruptor, the wrench thrown into a well-oiled machine.

Disruption isn't necessarily flashy. It's subtle. It's the double movement—showing for the ball, dragging a marker, and then darting into a new space just as the press begins. It's the decoy run into a tighter zone to open the corridor for a teammate. It's the disguised body shape that suggests a backwards pass, only for the ball to be zipped into the half-space on the turn.

The 8.5 operates largely in cognitive spaces. They manipulate defenders' decisions. A simple shoulder drop can trigger a press from the wrong angle. A feint backwards causes an opponent to bite, only for the ball to go forward. These are not coincidences. They're traps.

You've probably heard commentators say, *"He found space."* That's not accurate. The best 8.5s don't find space. They *manufacture* it. They pull a winger inside with a wall pass, rotate with an inverted full-back, and suddenly there's a 5v4 on the right flank. The defensive block has shifted. It's no longer a block—it's a puzzle with a missing piece.

Look at how Ilkay Gündoğan operates when Man City play against a low block. He doesn't just wait for space to appear. He makes it appear. By dragging a pivot forward, he opens a passing lane to the striker. By receiving with one foot and turning with the other, he accelerates the tempo. And once the tempo is up, the block begins to sway like a bridge in the wind.

Context matters too. Against a mid-block, the 8.5 will play higher—almost level with the forward line—to pin the second line of pressure deeper. Against a deep block, they'll drop to collect and recycle possession, luring out midfielders who've been instructed to stay compact. The role is elastic. It stretches and contracts based on the needs of the system.

If you're coaching or analysing, this is where you focus your lens—not on the flashy assist, but on the three movements that made it possible. Watch the way the 8.5 pulls a full-back just two metres central, opening a lane for the winger to receive on the run. That's not coincidence. That's choreography.

This type of possession play is not taught in isolation drills. It's developed in small-sided possession games with directional constraints, under time pressure, with multiple tasks. You train your 8.5 to scan, to move, to think three passes ahead. You don't want a specialist. You want a connector, a disruptor, a tempo-setter.

In elite football, those who control the middle third control the match. But it's not just about territory. It's about timing. The 8.5 doesn't dominate space—they manipulate time. They accelerate when the defence is static. They pause when the press is coming. They inject chaos just when the opposition thinks they've stabilised.

So, if you're evaluating a player, don't just track their completed passes. Track when and where those passes occur. Are they breaking defensive lines? Are they pulling markers? Are they increasing the tempo in the final third? That's where the true value lies.

The 8.5 in possession isn't just a role—it's a responsibility. You're not just progressing the ball. You're progressing the system. And if you do it well enough, the opposition's shape starts breaking down before they even realise it. That's when the game is won—not in the box, but in the spaces before the box, in the milliseconds before the final action.

And that's where you live. Right there. Between lines, between moments, between expectations.

Supporting the Build-Up

The build-up phase is where the hybrid midfielder—the 8.5—starts to show their real worth. It's the connective tissue between structure and spontaneity, and too often misunderstood as a place for safe passes and static geometry. In reality, it's where tactical intelligence meets spatial navigation. The 8.5 isn't just a receiver in this phase—they're a constructor of moments.

Let's walk through three elements that define the 8.5's role during build-up: **creating passing angles, dropping to assist pivots, and rotating with full-backs.** This isn't about heroic dribbles or defence-splitting assists. It's about the subtle movements that shift the entire chessboard.

Creating Passing Angles

The first thing you've got to understand about the 8.5 during build-up is this: they're not waiting to get the ball—they're working to become the best option.

That means constantly adjusting to create angles, not just for themselves, but for teammates. Think of it less as making yourself *"available"* and more like engineering visibility. The 8.5 lives between opposition lines, but in build-up, they often step into the shadows behind the first press, occupying what coaches call *"layer two."* Not quite a pivot, not quite an advanced midfielder. Just far enough to dodge pressure, just close enough to accelerate the next phase.

Watch players like İlkay Gündoğan or Bernardo Silva when their team builds from deep. They don't demand the ball with exaggerated gestures—they glide into spaces that draw the eyes of defenders while simultaneously offering their centre-backs or pivots an escape hatch. These angles aren't always forward-facing. Sometimes, a lateral or diagonal pass is the true accelerant. A backwards pass that unhinges a man-marking press can be more valuable than a forced vertical one.

The 8.5 isn't just collecting passes—they're designing routes. You'll see them slightly adjust their positioning to offer a better passing lane, often between the lines or just beyond the reach of a midfielder closing in. They'll step wide to stretch a compact block or drop inside to collapse a press trap. Every movement is functional, not flamboyant.

This ability to manipulate angles also allows the 8.5 to become a relay point between players who otherwise wouldn't be directly connected—the full-back and the striker, for instance, or the centre-back and the winger. In some systems, the 8.5's positioning helps bypass the pivot entirely, offering a secondary build-up lane that keeps the opposition guessing.

It's not about hiding in space. It's about curating it.

Dropping to Assist Pivots

Certain midfielders wait for the game to come to them. The 8.5? They go find the game.

In a possession-based system, especially one that builds from the back, pressure is inevitable. Whether it's a high press from a 4-4-2 or a mid-block with trap triggers, modern defences are designed to suffocate pivots. When that happens, the 8.5 becomes a pressure valve—dropping into deeper zones not to take over, but to collaborate.

This isn't a double pivot. This is relational positioning. The 8.5 drops as needed, not by default.

You'll notice it in teams like Manchester City. The 8.5 will peel away from their marker to create a temporary 2v1 with the pivot. That doesn't mean they stay deep. They're there to help create numerical superiority, receive under pressure, and then accelerate the play forward. It's a three-second intervention, not a positional shift.

The mistake many young players make is treating this drop as a retreat. It's not. It's an offensive move made from a defensive zone. When you drop, you're not abandoning your attacking duties—you're enabling them.

This is particularly crucial when facing man-oriented pressing schemes. If the 8.5 can drop into a line where no one follows them, they become a free man. If someone does follow, it creates a ripple effect—pulling shape, opening space, triggering rotations. Either way, the team wins.

The key here is timing. Drop too early, and you clutter the pivot lanes. Drop too late, and the press has already isolated your teammates. The elite 8.5s have an internal metronome

66

that matches the ball's rhythm, not just the opponent's pressure.

And when they do drop, it's not just to receive and release. It's to scan, turn, and build. An 8.5 should always be looking over their shoulder before the ball arrives, mapping the next pass before the first touch. This scanning behaviour turns reactive football into proactive orchestration.

Essentially, when done right, the 8.5's drop doesn't stall the build-up—it turbocharges it.

Rotating with Full-Backs

This is where the 8.5 starts to blur into the modernist—part midfielder, part wide connector, part orchestrator.

You've probably heard coaches talk about *"positional play"* and *"occupying the five lanes."*

If those terms sound unfamiliar, my book **Positionism** will walk you through them—and much more. This is where you see it in action. In teams that use inverted full-backs or asymmetric shapes, the 8.5 often rotates with wide defenders to maintain structural integrity. It's not about filling in—it's about rebalancing the system in real-time.

Rotation doesn't mean switching roles permanently. It means adapting to momentary needs. When a full-back inverts into midfield, the 8.5 might drift wide to prevent congestion. When a winger cuts inside, the 8.5 might overlap to stretch the pitch. These are micro-adjustments that require both tactical intelligence and real-time communication.

Think of how Liverpool's midfielders interact with Trent Alexander-Arnold when he steps into midfield. Or how Paris Saint-Germain's interiors rotate depending on what Achraf Hakimi is doing. These aren't rehearsed movements—they're instinctive responses to fluid shapes. And the 8.5 must be fluent in that language.

This rotation also has a defensive dimension. When full-backs push high, the 8.5 often tucks in to cover vacated zones, especially in sides that use a rest-defence shape of 2-3-5. If the ball is lost, the 8.5's positioning becomes crucial in stopping transitions. They're both the springboard and the seatbelt.

What separates the average from the elite in this regard is the understanding of when to rotate and when to hold. It's easy to chase balance and end up disconnected. The 8.5 must read not just their own line, but the entire tactical puzzle. Are the centre-backs split wide? Has the pivot shifted to the weak side? Has the winger stayed high or tucked in? Every decision is a response to those signals.

And this is where coaching matters. Top managers train these rotations with constraints—small-sided games where players are forced to solve spatial puzzles under pressure. But even with the best training, it comes down to the individual's ability to read the game like a living map.

There's also a psychological layer here. The best 8.5s don't see these rotations as chores. They see them as power plays. By rotating effectively, they increase their touches, their influence, and their ability to dictate tempo. They're not being unselfish—they're being dominant through adaptability.

In a world where tactical systems are becoming more fluid and less fixed, this capacity to rotate without fracturing structure is essential. The 8.5 isn't a cog—they're the gyroscope.

In the build-up phase, the 8.5 doesn't just support. They sculpt. They carve out angles, collaborate under pressure, and rotate with rhythm. This isn't a role for the passive or positional. It's for the midfielder who wants to own the tempo, not just follow it. The 8.5 doesn't wait for the game to develop—they build it, brick by brick.

Final Third Influence

There's a moment in every match where the midfield fades into the background. The crowd is focused on the striker, the winger bursting down the flank, the ball zipping toward goal. But go back a few seconds. Rewind the move. Who timed the run that disrupted the back line? Who shaped the pass that split defenders without even touching the ball? That's where the 8.5 lives. Their fingerprints are on the goal, even if the statisticians miss it. In the final third, the hybrid midfielder becomes the shadow architect. Not always the scorer, not always the assister—but usually the reason it all clicked.

Arriving Late in the Box

You don't need to be the fastest player to beat a back line. You just need to be later than expected. Arriving late in the box is one of the 8.5's most lethal weapons. It's also one of the most misunderstood.

Traditional forwards operate on the shoulder of the last defender. Their job is to stretch, pin, and pounce. The 8.5? They move like smoke. They hover between the lines, then time their arrival so they're unmarked when the ball is cut back. You're not sprinting into the box with a neon sign saying *"MARK ME."* You're lurking. Watching. Then moving when the defenders glance away or get dragged by more obvious threats.

Think Frank Lampard in his prime. He wasn't the most athletic midfielder in the league. But he mastered the art of timing. He studied his teammates' tendencies. Knew when the winger would deliver. Knew where the ball would be cut back. And crucially, he knew when to hold and when to burst.

As a coach, this is something you can train. Set up a rondo-style drill but with a finish. Let the 8.5 start outside the box, then trigger their movement based on a passing cue or a defender's movement. Repeat it until it becomes instinctive. As a player, study video. Not of the goals, but the 3–5 seconds before. Where was the midfielder? What did they read in the defence?

Late arrivals create chaos because defenders are ball-watching or man-marking the obvious threats. The 8.5 exploits that momentary lapse. It's not flair—it's cold, clinical timing.

Linking with Forwards

Linking up isn't about pinging wall passes or playing Hollywood flicks. It's about understanding tempo. The 8.5 is the rhythm guitarist in a band full of soloists. You set the pace, the groove, the transitions between chaos and control.

You're not duplicating the number 10's job—you're complementing it. If your striker drops deep, you run beyond. If they spin in behind, you show short. It's the constant rebalancing act of vertical harmony. You're the glue between midfield build-up and attacking execution.

Great 8.5s don't just combine with the striker—they speak the same football language. Think of how elite creators like Kevin De Bruyne have connected with dynamic forwards like Erling Haaland—passing not to where the striker is, but to the run that hasn't even started yet. That's not extra-sensory perception—it's pattern recognition, tactical chemistry, and hours of training.

You need to build that intuition. Play small-sided games with your forwards. Force combinations in tight spaces. Set constraints where the only route to goal is a third-man run or a layoff. You're not just sharpening skills—you're learning habits, preferences, blind-spot awareness.

And don't forget communication. Non-verbal cues matter. A glance. A shoulder drop. A quick hand point. These are micro-signals that unlock defences. The 8.5 who masters them becomes indispensable—not because they dominate the ball, but because they make everyone else's job easier.

In modern systems, the 8.5 might even be the one initiating the press immediately after a failed final-third entry. Your job isn't done once the ball leaves your foot. You're reading the next phase before it starts.

Making Decoy Runs to Open Space

Here's where it gets beautifully counterintuitive: sometimes, your best move is the one that doesn't involve the ball at all. Decoy runs are the secret sauce of elite movement. You're not making a run to receive—you're making a run to manipulate.

A well-timed decoy run pulls defenders out of structure. It creates gaps for others to exploit. And the best part? You don't need the ball to control the game.

Watch Thomas Müller and you'll understand the concept of the Raumdeuter—*"space interpreter."* He doesn't operate in traditional zones. He finds the cracks. And more importantly, he creates them. Müller often pulls centre-backs wide, not to receive, but to clear a channel for a late-arriving midfielder or inverted winger. It's selfless. It's tactical. And it's devastatingly effective.

As the 8.5, you are uniquely positioned to make these vertical-lateral runs. You're not shackled to the touchline or pinned to the pivot. You float. That freedom allows you to drag markers, overload flanks, or even run diagonally to trigger a rotation elsewhere on the pitch.

In training, simulate these scenarios. Use mannequins or cones to represent defensive lines. Practise curved runs that start centrally and arc wide. Or shallow runs that pull a full-back in, only for the winger to dart behind. It's cat-and-mouse, and you're the one holding the string.

The real magic? These runs often go unnoticed by casual fans or surface-level analysis. There's no stat for *"created space by not touching the ball."* But analysts and coaches know. They see the domino effect. They see how your off-ball intelligence opens up entire tactical pathways.

If you're a player looking to level up, start watching matches with a different lens. Don't follow the ball. Track the midfielders off it. Who's making space? Who's dragging defenders? Who's affecting the game without demanding the spotlight?

As a coach, reward these actions. Clip them. Show them in film sessions. Praise the decoy run that led to the goal, not just the assist. Build a culture where unselfish movement is celebrated, not ignored.

Because in the final third, the 8.5 isn't just a connector or a technician. They're a spatial engineer. A manipulator of attention. A ghost that haunts defenders not by presence—but by absence.

And that's where the modern game is headed. Not more touches. Smarter ones. Not more runs. Better-timed ones. Not more goals. But goals that start three passes before the assist, orchestrated by a midfielder who never needed the limelight to control the narrative.

6

The 8.5 Out of Possession: The Art of Anticipation

Pressing Principles

In the rhythm of modern football, pressing is no longer a luxury—it's a necessity. It's the defensive equivalent of jazz: structured chaos, synchronised aggression, and a deep understanding between players who must operate as one. And at the heart of this symphony? The 8.5.

You're not just looking for someone who can run. You're looking for someone who can read. Someone who sees the trap before it's sprung, and ideally, helps set it. The 8.5 is the architect of the midfield press, the player who initiates the moment of collective suffocation that turns defence into attack.

Let's break it down.

Leading the Press from Midfield

Forget the static midfield blocks of old. The modern 8.5 presses like a predator—disguised, patient, then explosive. While the traditional No. 6 might hold shape behind the play, and the pure 10 waits for the ball further up, the 8.5 is the one who reads both the opponent's build-up and their body language.

Your role here isn't just to follow instructions; it's to interpret the flow of the game in real-time. The best 8.5s don't wait for a coach's signal—they press based on cues they've internalised: a heavy touch, a sideways pass, a moment of isolation. You're not just reacting, you're dictating.

Think of players like Jude Bellingham at Real Madrid or Gavi at Barcelona. These aren't just workhorses—they're intelligent pressers who know when to go and, more importantly, when not to. The 8.5 initiates the squeeze, not with reckless energy, but with a chess player's precision.

And this is where pressing becomes psychological warfare. When the 8.5 steps forward, it sends a message: we're not waiting. We're taking control of your build-up. That kind of mentality ripples through the team.

Trigger-Based Engagements

Pressing isn't random. It's choreographed. And the 8.5 is often the trigger. It might be the opponent's pass into the full-back. It might be a back pass that invites pressure. It might even be a keeper receiving the ball on his weaker foot.

What separates a good pressing side from a great one is how they disguise the moment before the ambush. The 8.5 floats in space, not always tightly marking, but shadowing passing lanes, baiting the opposition to take the 'safe' option. Then comes the snap.

You're not just chasing the ball—you're herding the opponent into a zone where your team has numerical superiority. This is where the 8.5's spatial awareness becomes critical. You must know where your winger is, where your pivot sits, and whether your striker is ready to cut off the return pass.

A properly timed press from the 8.5 can collapse an entire possession phase. It's like pulling a thread and watching the whole jumper unravel. When you get it right, the reward is brutal—high regains, unbalanced opponents, and transition moments in dangerous zones.

And here's the nuance: you don't always press full throttle. Sometimes, the 8.5 shows restraint to channel the play into a trap. Sometimes, you slow the opponent just long enough for your teammates to reset. Pressing isn't just about energy—it's about control.

Coordinating with the Attacking Line

Now, here's where things get beautifully complex. Pressing from midfield only works if you're in sync with the front line. And this is where the hybrid nature of the 8.5 shines. You're not operating in isolation—you're the bridge between forwards and deeper midfielders.

When the striker curves his run to block the centre-back's passing lane, your job is to mirror that movement. If the winger cuts inward to press the full-back, you shift diagonally to block the escape route through the pivot.

You're not just pressing—you're boxing in. The best teams don't let the opponent breathe because their lines move in harmony. And you, as the 8.5, are the connective tissue.

This is where role fluidity becomes more than a buzzword. If you're pressing as a No. 8 and the winger tucks inside, you might drift wider to cover. If the striker drops to press the pivot, you step up higher. The lines blur, but the structure remains.

In a high-functioning press, the 8.5 becomes a controller without the ball. You're dictating space, tempo, and decision-making for the opposition. That's the kind of influence that rarely shows up on stat sheets but defines elite-level football.

One final element: *communication*. The 8.5 must constantly talk. You're not just executing actions—you're orchestrating reactions. A subtle hand gesture, a quick shout to the winger, a glance at the centre-back—this is how pressing units stay connected.

The 8.5 doesn't just press to win the ball. You press to shape the game.

And the best part? When the opponent finally coughs up possession under your pressure, you're already in the zone that matters—the middle third. Unlike a winger who's recovering or a full-back who's out wide, you're in the corridor of consequence. One pass, one drive, and you're launching the next attack.

That's the beauty of the 8.5 out of possession. You're everywhere. And more importantly, you're exactly where the game is about to tilt.

Defensive Recovery

There's a moment—right after the ball is lost—when everything hangs in the balance. The opponents smell blood, the crowd holds its breath, and the system you've worked all week on is at its most vulnerable. For the hybrid 8.5, this is where the game starts again. Defensive recovery isn't a retroactive scramble—it's proactive anticipation. It's knowing how to cover space vacated by others, tracking the right runners, and breaking up transitions before they bloom. It's not glamorous. But it's decisive.

The best 8.5s are not just creators in attack—they are destroyers in disguise when out of possession. This is where the double-life becomes real: the same player who split the lines with a pass seconds ago is now preventing a counter that could undo it all.

Let's break this down into three key responsibilities.

Covering Vacated Full-Back Zones

Modern full-backs are now auxiliary wingers. They invert, they bomb forward, they join central build-ups. This aggressive positioning creates overloads—and, inevitably, vulnerabilities. When that full-back is caught high and wide, someone has to plug the hole.

Enter the 8.5.

You're not a full-back. You're not even pretending to be. But when your left-back has pushed into the half-space or high touchline, and you lose the ball, that zone becomes a bullseye. Opposition wingers or attacking mids are trained to exploit that gap instantly. If you're a true 8.5, you've already seen it coming.

Recovery here isn't about chasing shadows—it's about understanding shape. You slide laterally, read the trigger (usually a turnover in the middle third), and drop into the channel. You don't commit to a tackle unless you're certain. Your job is to delay, contain, and funnel. Buy time for your full-back to recover or force the opponent into a less threatening zone.

Players like Joshua Kimmich and Declan Rice understand this intuitively. They don't just run—they fill space with purpose. Covering a vacated flank isn't about marking a man; it's about temporarily becoming the system's glue. You restore balance by plugging the temporary void. It's the footballing equivalent of sealing a leak before the boat floods.

A coach doesn't always draw this on a whiteboard. This is the kind of recovery that lives in the grey space of game intelligence. You either see it and move—or you don't, and your team gets punished.

Tracking Central Runners

This is the test of your mental RPM. In the chaos of transition, it's not always the ball-carrier who kills you—it's the late-arriving runner. The one you didn't see because you were ball-watching. The one sprinting from deep behind the striker, ghosting into your defensive third. The one who was your responsibility.

This is where the 8.5 earns their credibility. Not by chasing the ball like a headless pressing machine, but by clocking who's breaking lines behind them. It's a subtle skill—reading body angles of opponents, listening for teammates' shouts, and scanning constantly. The best 8.5s are those who know the run is coming before it even starts.

You don't need to win the ball here. You need to make the run harder. Stay goal-side. Apply just enough pressure that their timing is disrupted. A half-second delay can be the difference between a cutback and an interception. This is not reactive defending—this is preventative marking.

Elite teams are filled with runners. Think Jude Bellingham. Think Nicolo Barella. These are players who don't stay static— they time their movement to perfection. You, as the 8.5, need to be the one player who recognises the trigger and tracks it. If you're caught ball-watching, you're toast. If you're proactive, you cut off the supply line.

There's also a psychological component here. Midfielders who track back effectively demoralise opponents. You force them to recycle the ball, to reset, to think twice about exploiting that same channel again. It's a subtle battle of attrition—and you win it by consistently being where they don't want you to be.

Breaking up Counter-Attacks

This is the dark art. Not the lung-busting sprint back—that's only the physical layer. The deeper layer is decision-making: when to foul, when to delay, and when to engage. Break up the counter, and you reset the chessboard. Let it run, and you're a pawn watching the king fall.

The 8.5 isn't always the deepest midfielder, but he's often the first line of midfield resistance. That matters. You're the player closest to the turnover. That means you're the first to challenge the immediate outlet. If you can't win the ball, you slow the play. If you can't slow the play, you foul smartly. If fouling isn't an option? Channel the run wide and delay.

Look at players like Leon Goretzka or Federico Valverde. They don't just run—they intercept. They don't just tackle—they manipulate space. They funnel counters into less threatening zones. They know when to take the yellow card. Not out of malice, but out of tactical maturity.

A solid 8.5 knows that not all counter-attacks are created equal. Some are recoverable with team shape. Others are lethal and must be stopped at the root. That discernment—knowing when the danger is existential—is where you separate the good from the elite.

This part of the role is about tempo control. You can't always dominate the ball, but you can dominate the rhythm of the game. Break up the counter, and you take back control of the tempo. You force the opposition to attack against your set shape, not your scattered pieces.

The 8.5's defensive recovery role is not about hero moments. It's about consistency. You're not chasing glory—you're preserving structure. Think of yourself as a stabiliser. When the system lurches from losing the ball, you're the one who ensures it doesn't collapse.

Recovery isn't just physical—it's spatial awareness at a sprint. It's knowing who's behind you, who's to your left, and what the opposition intend to do next. It's not intuition. It's trained instinct. And it's what makes the hybrid midfielder such a rare and valuable breed.

You can't fake this part of the game. You either anticipate or you chase. And in the highest levels of football, the difference between those two is the difference between a clean sheet and a concession. Between a win and a 2-2 draw. Between lifting a trophy and nearly lifting it.

Spatial Discipline

There's a moment in every high-stakes match where the camera pans out just enough to show the entire midfield line shifting in unison—silent, synchronised, and subtle. It's in that moment where you can see the 8.5's true value: not in flashy feints or clever flicks, but in shape, structure, and spacing. Spatial discipline isn't glamorous. It's not going to sell shirts or trend on Twitter. But it's what separates the tactically literate from the tactically elite.

You're not just chasing the ball. You're managing space. You're not just tracking runners. You're anticipating danger. You're not just defending. You're making sure the team doesn't fall apart when the ball is lost. And in that fragile in-between where chaos looms, the 8.5 becomes the anchor, the orchestrator of spatial integrity.

Let's break down what that actually means in the heat of battle.

Holding Shape in Transition

Transitions are where games are won and lost. That's not an exaggeration. The 8.5 lives in the eye of the storm—between the moment possession is lost and shape is regained. The instinct for many players is to rush toward the ball or to instantly press the nearest opponent. But the 8.5 has to resist that urge. You're playing chess while others are playing pinball.

Holding shape isn't about standing still. It's about calculated movement. When your team loses possession, your first job isn't always to press—it's to scan. Where are the gaps? Where are the opposition's outlets? Are your full-backs caught high? Is your pivot isolated? You have one or two seconds to assess, adjust, and act.

Coaches often talk about *"rest defence"* — your team's structure in possession that prepares you for the moment you lose the ball. The 8.5 is central to that. If you've positioned yourself correctly—slightly tucked in, with access to central and half-space zones—you're already halfway to controlling the transition. If you're too high, too wide, or too eager to join the attack, you've created a vacuum. The kind that counter-attacks love to fill.

It's not just about where you are. It's about where you're not. You need to be in the place that stops the pass that breaks the press. You need to be the cover shadow behind the forward press. You need to be the player who slows the game down just enough for your teammates to recover. That's not something you'll see in the match stats, but it's the kind of action that turns a five-second sprint into a five-pass reset.

Controlling Central Corridors

Central corridors are sacred. No team wants to concede space down the middle—it's the red carpet to goal. And yet, it's astonishing how often this area becomes exposed, especially when teams play with attacking midfielders who don't track back or with double pivots that drift apart.

The 8.5 is the insurance policy against that exposure. You're not a destroyer like a classic 6, and you're not a pure creator like a 10. But you are the gatekeeper. You control the lanes between the lines.

Let's talk spacing. The best 8.5s operate in vertical channels between the pivot and the front line. They float in the seam—not too close to the centre-backs to clog the build-up, not too close to the forwards to be bypassed in transition. It's a Goldilocks zone, and it requires constant recalibration.

When the opposition attacks through the middle, your role is twofold: delay and direct. You delay the pass by positioning your body to cut off angles. You direct the opposition by showing them into wider zones where your team has more cover. Think of yourself as a funnel—not a wall. You're not trying to win every duel; you're trying to guide the play into areas where the odds are in your favour.

Watch how top-level 8.5s like Ilkay Gündoğan or Frenkie de Jong operate without touching the ball. Their hips are angled to block one pass and bait another. They shift two yards to the left, and suddenly the opposition's perfect passing lane evaporates. That's spatial control. That's defensive intelligence.

You also need to understand when to step and when to screen. If the ball enters your zone with a receiver in a poor body position, step and press. But if the receiver is facing forward with options, your job is to screen—create time for your teammates to get set, and make sure any forward pass has to go around you, not through you.

Blocking Passing Lanes

There's a reason top coaches obsess over body orientation. The way you angle your shoulders can open or close entire channels of play. Blocking passing lanes is an art form, and for the hybrid midfielder, it's non-negotiable.

It starts with scanning. You need to know where the ball is, where the next pass might go, and where the opposition's danger players are lurking. Think of it as a three-point triangle: ball, passing lane, and receiver. Your positioning should bisect that triangle. That's how you cut off options without chasing shadows.

You're not just standing in the way—you're manipulating the opponent's decisions. When you position yourself between the centre-back and the pivot, you're saying: *"Try the risky pass through me, or go wide and let us reset."* When you shift a few steps to cut off the inside pass, you're forcing them back or sideways. Every metre they lose is a metre your team gains in time and structure.

Blocking lanes also requires discipline. You'll be tempted to dive in, especially when the ball is close. But the best 8.5s know when to stay passive. You're not hunting the ball; you're shepherding the options. Let the opposition have the ball if it means they can't do anything dangerous with it.

There's nuance here. You're not always cutting off the closest option. Sometimes, you block the second pass—the one that breaks the lines. You're thinking two moves ahead. If the ball goes to the full-back, and you know they want to bounce it inside to a free 10, your job is to block that second pass before it's even played.

In modern pressing systems, this becomes even more critical.

85

When your team triggers a press, your job is to close the lane that leads to the escape route. You're the safety net behind the trigger. If you don't get your angle right, the whole press collapses.

And here's the brutal truth: no one will thank you for it. Your name won't be in the highlights, and the commentators won't mention your positioning. But your coach will see it. The analyst will clip it. And the team will feel it.

The 8.5 isn't just a connector. You're the midfield's firewall. In the chaos of transition, when the tactical plan frays and opponents try to exploit disorganisation, your spatial discipline is what puts out the fire before it spreads.

You're not just playing against players. You're playing against systems, triggers, and patterns. Every step you take, every angle you hold, every lane you close—it all feeds into the collective shape. And when that shape holds? That's when the whole team breathes easier. That's when you know you've done your job.

7

The Double-Life of the 8.5: Attacker or Midfielder?

Half-Space Dynamics

The half-space is where tactical nuance meets creative chaos. It's the corridor between the centre and the wing — not quite one, not entirely the other. If you watch elite-level football with an analytical eye, this is where your gaze will gravitate. Why? Because it's where the game breathes — and often where it breaks.

The 8.5 lives here. Not visits. Lives.

They operate in these ambiguous lanes, constantly interpreting the flow of the match. They aren't shackled to one zone, nor do they linger in the limelight like a traditional number 10. Instead, they thrive in these grey zones — where defenders are uncertain, and spaces are transient.

To fully understand the tactical gravity of the 8.5 in the half-space, you have to appreciate how they weaponise ambiguity.

Operating in the Grey Zones

Here's what you don't see on the stats sheet: the subtle movement that draws a pivot wide, the half-second delay before checking into space, the shoulder feint that freezes a pressing full-back. The 8.5 is a master of deception and timing, not just execution.

In a 4-3-3 or when building into a 3-2-5 shape, watch where the interior midfielders drift. They're not hugging the touchline or standing on the toes of the striker. They're lurking — between the lines of the opposition's midfield and defence, in the blind spot of a centre-back, just outside the pressing arc of a holding midfielder.

You'll see them receive on the half-turn, body angled diagonally, eyes scanning diagonally across the pitch. Why? Because the half-space offers them three directions of play: *inside, outside, and forward.* From here, they can slip a through ball, combine with an overlapping full-back, or recycle possession with a pivot behind. This connectivity is the lifeblood of positional play.

But it's not just about receiving. It's about attracting. The best 8.5s don't just find space — they create it. By holding their run for a fraction longer, they pull the defensive shape towards them. That creates pockets elsewhere. Wingers benefit, strikers gain half-yards, and full-backs can invert or overlap with more conviction.

Watch Martin Ødegaard at Arsenal. He doesn't just play in the half-space; he bends the game around it.

Creating 2v1s with Wingers and Full-Backs

The half-space is a cheat code when you learn how to manipulate it with others. The 8.5 thrives in creating temporary numerical advantages — not through brute force, but through positioning and tempo.

On the right side, imagine the 8.5 linking with the winger and the full-back. The triangle becomes a dynamic organism — fluid, rotating, overloading. One drops, one goes, the other pivots. The goal isn't just to beat a man, but to destabilise the structure.

When the 8.5 drifts wide and the winger inverts, the opponent's full-back is caught between decisions. Stay tight to the winger and leave the 8.5? Step out to press and expose the channel? This uncertainty is where the 8.5 feasts.

In a 3-2-5 structure, the 8.5 often operates just ahead of the double pivot and just inside the wing-back. This positioning invites overloads in the wide channel without sacrificing central presence. It's not just about wide play — it's about drawing opposition midfielders into uncomfortable zones, unbalancing them, and exploiting the seams that open up.

You'll often see the 8.5 execute a third-man combination: play into the winger, who lays off to the overlapping full-back, while the 8.5 darts into the box. It's not a scripted move. It's instinct meets structure.

This isn't tiki-taka for the sake of it. It's targeted, timed disruption.

Exploiting the Blindside

The blindside is where defenders lose track of movement. It's the space behind the shoulder, the moment when a player looks one way and the 8.5 ghosts in the other.

Great 8.5s don't always demand the ball in open space. They arrive in it.

This is what separates them from a traditional number 10. They don't operate in static pockets, waiting for a defence-splitting pass. They manipulate the timing of their runs, often starting from a deeper midfield position, then accelerating into the attacking third when the line is distracted.

Think of a centre-back focusing on the striker and suddenly the 8.5 appears just behind them. Or a defensive midfielder stepping toward the ball, only to find the 8.5 has slipped into the space they left behind. These are not accidents — they are engineered moments of disorganisation.

To exploit the blindside, the 8.5 must have elite scanning habits. Before the ball is played, they know where the gaps are, where the defenders are leaning, and where the next action might occur. This is neurological football — fast processing, layered decision-making, and seamless execution.

Kevin De Bruyne is the master of this. Watch how often he arrives in the channel unmarked, not because he's quick, but because he's unseen. Blindside runs aren't about speed. They're about perception — yours versus the opponent's.

And when the 8.5 does get the ball in these moments, the options multiply. A cutback. A low cross. A disguised pass to the edge of the box. Or — if the moment calls — a driven strike into the far corner. The decision depends on the game state, the teammate's movement, and the opponent's positioning. But the moment itself? That was created in the half-space, on the blindside, without fanfare.

The 8.5 doesn't need to be the star. But they are the accelerant.

In teams that dominate possession, the 8.5 is less about goals and assists, more about tempo and control. In teams built to transition, they become the conduit — the one who arrives late but leaves early, initiating counters with one-touch layoffs or third-man runs that upend defensive structures.

When you see a goal scored after four quick passes, remember who started it. Not with a flashy flick or a no-look pass. But with a subtle find of space, a clever body angle, a perfectly weighted touch.

The 8.5 lives in the shadows of the tactical map, but their influence is seismic. They don't just play between the lines. They redefine them.

So next time you're watching a match, don't follow the ball. Follow the player who's never standing still, always scanning, and constantly nudging defenders into zones they don't want to be in. That's your 8.5. And they're not an attacker. They're not a midfielder. They're both — and neither.

They're the ghost in the system. And the system bends when they move.

Shadow Striker Tendencies

The most dangerous players on the pitch rarely play where you expect them to. That's the essence of the 8.5 when they slip into the shadow striker mode—part ghost, part predator. They don't need to be labelled as forwards to destroy defensive structures. They find the cracks, the hesitations, the half-a-second when a centre-back glances over his shoulder and realises... no one's there, but somehow the net is rippling.

This is where the 8.5 becomes something else entirely. Not quite a 10, definitely not a pure 9, but a hybrid who reads the emotional rhythm of a match and inserts chaos precisely where structure is most fragile.

Ghosting into the Box

You don't need to be the fastest player on the pitch to arrive first in the box. It's about timing. It's about sensing the tempo of an attack and moving two seconds before the defender even considers looking over his shoulder. Ghosting runs are a psychological weapon—they punish defenders who ball-watch, who hesitate, who track space instead of men.

The classic late arrival into the area isn't just about attacking instinct; it's about creating a mismatch. While the forwards pin the centre-backs and the wingers stretch the full-backs, the 8.5 finds the seam between the lines. You're not the focal point of the attack, and that's exactly the point. You're the secondary threat defenders clock too late.

Think about players like Thomas Müller in his Raumdeuter (space interpreter) phase, or Frank Lampard's absurd goal record for a midfielder. They weren't always on the shoulder of the last man. They were arriving from deep, undetected, into zones the defence had no cover for. When you ghost into the box, you arrive with momentum, with vision, and often with the element of surprise. And in elite football, surprise is currency.

Coaches looking to develop this trait in their midfielders should focus on timing and second-phase movement. It's not about sprinting into the box on every attack—it's about recognising when the defensive line is distracted or disorganised and stepping into the chaos. Drills that simulate delayed runs, late entries from midfield, and finishing from the edge of the area in crowded boxes can hardwire this instinct.

Acting as a Secondary Forward

The 8.5 doesn't just support the attack—they can become the attack. In systems where a single striker leads the line, the secondary forward becomes essential in creating vertical partnerships. Especially when facing a back four, the extra runner from deep forces centre-backs into decisions they don't want to make: step out and risk opening space behind, or hold the line and let the midfielder receive in dangerous areas.

You're not playing with a front two, but you're creating the effect of one. The beauty of this hybrid role is that it doesn't need to be static. You can engage in rotations with the striker, overload the box when the opportunity arises, or drift into channels to stretch the defence horizontally.

Look at players like Kai Havertz. He's not a traditional striker, nor a classic 10. But in attacking phases, he lives in the pockets defenders hate to defend. He offers an outlet through decoy runs and secondary threats that bend defensive lines out of shape.

In training scenarios, you can replicate this by using overload drills in the final third that force defenders to track both a striker and a deep runner. Encourage midfielders to make runs beyond the striker, not just support from deep. It's about creating a psychological edge—defenders must constantly check who's around them, not just ahead of them.

And for analysts and scouts, this is where modern data can be deceptive. A midfielder may not have high expected goals (xG) numbers, but if they consistently make high-value secondary runs—pulling markers, creating overloads, drawing fouls in advanced areas—they're adding invisible value to the attacking structure. Track movement data, not just touches or passes.

Capitalising on Chaos

Football rarely breaks down in neat patterns. Matches are messy. Structures collapse, rebounds fall unpredictably, defenders slip, and clearances fall short. This is where the 8.5 thrives—not in orchestrating the perfect move, but in being the first to react when the game disintegrates.

You need to develop a nose for chaos. It's like a sixth sense—knowing when a deflected shot will fall in the six-yard box, when a centre-back's heavy touch will offer a split-second chance to pounce, or when a defensive midfielder misjudges the tempo of a recycled ball. The 8.5 doesn't just read these moments—they act on them.

And more importantly, they position themselves in areas where chaos is most likely to occur. Not hugging the penalty spot, but lurking near the penalty arc. Not chasing the first ball in, but anticipating the second. It's about positioning yourself at the tipping point of mayhem, where a single touch can lead to a goal or a goal-saving tackle.

Players like Ilkay Gündoğan have made a living off this trait. His goals often come not from flashy dribbles or long-range strikes, but from being in the right place at the wrong time—for the opponent. He arrives when the game is in flux, when the structure is gone, and the defenders are reacting rather than controlling.

From a coaching perspective, small-sided games with quick transitions are gold here. Set up drills where midfielders must react to ricochets, second balls, and defensive breakdowns. Train anticipation as much as execution. It's about developing the ability to read the emotional temperature of the match—to know when the next five seconds will decide everything.

For players, this is not just about technical sharpness, but mental readiness. Chaos comes without warning. If you're too rigid, too structured, too obsessed with holding your zone, you'll miss the window. The 8.5 must live at the edge of structure, one foot in the system, one foot ready to abandon it if the opportunity demands.

And for analysts, there's a quiet revolution in tracking this. Ball recovery locations, heat maps during broken play phases, and off-ball movement in second-phase attacks are becoming essential. It's no longer enough to track completed passes or pass accuracy. You need to measure presence in chaos—who's there when the structure fails?

This, ultimately, is the essence of the shadow striker mode within the 8.5 role. It's not about being a luxury player. It's about being the connective tissue between midfield clarity and attacking improvisation. A player who can disappear from the marker's eye, reappear in the goalmouth, and leave analysts wondering: where did he come from?

Where the classic 9 finishes the move, the 8.5 finishes the mistake.

Midfield Responsibility

There's a reason the 8.5 isn't just another fancy number on a tactical chalkboard. This role is a balancing act—creative free-dom meets tactical discipline. It's the footballing equivalent of walking a tightrope while juggling chainsaws. You're not just there to float around and look pretty in the half-spaces; you're also expected to hold the midfield fabric together when the game turns chaotic. The 8.5 is a dual citizen in the final third and the engine room—*playmaker* and *anchor*, *artist* and *architect*.

Let's break it down into three key demands: *maintaining creative licence without losing structural integrity, rotating intelli-gently with the pivot*, and *consistently supporting transitions both ways*. These aren't buzzwords—they're the defining traits of a midfielder who doesn't just play between the lines, but thinks between them too.

Balancing Creative Freedom with Structure

You can't afford to be a luxury player. The days when a number 10 could stroll across the pitch waiting for the ball to arrive at their feet are long gone. In today's game, freedom is earned through reliability. The moment you lose positional discipline, the entire system starts cracking—especially when your team loses the ball.

Take Kevin De Bruyne. Yes, he racks up assists like it's a video game, but his real genius lies in his ability to sense when to drift and when to hold. He doesn't just chase space—he calculates risk. You have to know when your movement unlocks the opposition and when it unbalances your own side.

This starts with understanding your role in the build-up. You might be operating in the half-spaces, but if your pivot needs a short option to relieve pressure, you're expected to become that outlet. That doesn't mean dropping into a double-pivot every time, but you need to track the flow of the game and adjust accordingly.

Freedom comes with a non-negotiable: cover your zone defensively, and occupy smart spaces in possession. If you drift too wide, who's holding interior zones? If you push too high, who's linking play? These aren't philosophical questions—they're spatial dilemmas that define whether your team controls or chases the game.

In elite setups, coaches don't tell their 8.5s exactly where to be every second. They trust them to understand the game context: the opposition's shape, the moment of the match, the spacing of teammates. The game isn't scripted. It's jazz. You need to improvise without missing a beat.

Rotating with the Pivot

One of the least glamorous, most misunderstood aspects of the 8.5 role is rotational play with the pivot. It's not just about covering space—it's about creating angles, manipulating opposition pressing traps, and maintaining balance.

Here's what that means in practical terms: when the pivot gets pulled out by an aggressive press, you drop in. When the pivot is overloaded, you present a new angle to bypass the pressure. When the pivot steps forward into the final third (think Frenkie de Jong surging upfield), you instantly fill their space to prevent the dreaded midfield vacuum.

Rotation isn't a routine—it's a conversation. It's silent communication between players who understand timing, rhythm, and spacing. The best 8.5s develop a sixth sense for when their pivot is about to move. They don't wait for a shout or a gesture; they just know.

This is where your football IQ gets tested. You have to read the triggers—opposition pressing cues, your pivot's body language, the angles of full-backs and centre-backs. It's a mental load that doesn't show up in highlight reels but determines whether your team plays through the lines or gets boxed in.

There's also a psychological component. In many systems, the pivot is seen as the anchor, the metronome. For you to rotate with them effectively, you need to earn mutual trust. That means being positionally reliable, tactically aware, and technically secure. One bad rotation can expose your team to a counter, or worse—invite a goal.

And when the rotation clicks? You create an illusion of numerical superiority. Suddenly, it looks like your team has two pivots and two attacking midfielders. That's the magic of fluidity—it multiplies your presence without changing personnel.

Supporting Transitions Both Ways

This is where the 8.5 separates from traditional roles. You're not just a connector in possession; you're a catalyst when the ball turns over. Whether it's a recovery or a loss, the game pivots on transition—and that's your domain.

Let's start with offensive transitions. When your team regains the ball, you're not waiting for instructions. You're scanning before the regain, already plotting the next phase. Are the wide players isolated? Is there a diagonal switch available? Can your movement drag a marker to open space for a forward?

Speed matters, but so does direction. The best 8.5s don't just sprint—they vector. They choose the right angles to support the break. That could mean underlapping a winger, arriving late outside the box, or simply holding your run to offer a back-pass option if the transition stalls.

Now flip it. Defensive transitions are your stress test. You've just lost the ball. Are you reacting, or are you already in position? The 8.5 who can immediately drop into the second line and block central access buys their team crucial seconds to regroup. You don't always need to win the ball back yourself—you just need to delay the attack. Force the wide pass. Block the first channel. Cut the tempo.

What sets elite 8.5s apart is their anticipation. They don't wait for the turnover—they expect it. They read the body shape of the teammate on the ball, the positioning of the press, the likelihood of a miscontrol or interception. Then they move early.

Transitions are also where your engine matters. You're expected to make repeated high-intensity runs, often back-to-back. You can't afford a mental lag or a physical dip. One second of hesitation and the opposition is behind your midfield line.

This is where training meets intuition. Coaches can drill rest defence structures and pressing triggers, but it's on you to interpret each moment. You're not a robot executing patterns—you're an active node in a complex, fluid system. Your job is to stabilise chaos.

And here's the unspoken truth: the 8.5 is often the difference between a fast break and a failed one, a counter conceded and a counter launched. You're not just playing both sides of the ball—you're defining how quickly your team moves between them.

If you want the creative freedom to roam, to affect the final third, to ghost into the box and tally assists, you have to earn it by being tactically dependable. If you want the licence to drift, to rotate, to pop up in unpredictable zones, you have to master the art of balance. The modern game doesn't tolerate passengers—it rewards players who can operate in ambiguity, hold structure while breaking it, and move in concert with their team's tactical rhythm.

Being an 8.5 is less about filling a role and more about playing a responsibility. You're the hinge between formation and function, theory and execution, freedom and control. The more you understand that, the more influence you have—not just on the game, but on how the game is played.

8

Coaching the 8.5: Building from the Ground Up

Youth Development

You can spot it. That one kid in your academy session who doesn't fit into the usual categories. Not quite a number 10, too mobile to be a deep-lying 6, yet somehow always in the right place to link play, press intelligently, and arrive late in the box. This is your future 8.5 — that rare hybrid midfielder who thinks like a playmaker but moves like a box-to-box engine. The challenge: *how do you coach that player from the raw material of potential into the heartbeat of a top-level system?*

If you want to develop an 8.5, you have to start young. Not just young in age, but young in tactical identity. Before positional roles calcify. Before coaches shove a player into the *"he's a winger"* or *"she's a defensive mid"* box. The 8.5 thrives on ambiguity. You must train them to become comfortable with that.

Identifying Hybrid Potential Early

The traditional academy model loves clarity. Coaches classify early. Strikers finish. Defenders defend. Midfielders either break up play or pick passes. But the hybrid 8.5 breaks this binary model. You're looking for players who don't dominate a session with flashy 1v1s or Hollywood diagonals, but those who stitch everything together.

It starts with intelligence in space. Watch how a player scans before receiving. Count how often they receive the ball facing forward. Track their movements off the ball — do they float into the half-space naturally? Do they adjust their body shape to draw pressure away from a teammate? These aren't just "*nice*" traits. They're the seeds of a future system-optimiser.

You'll notice something else: these players often seem a step slower in drills but are two steps ahead in games. They aren't focused on winning the rondo. They're focused on where the next pass should go. That's your player.

And don't get fooled by physicality. At U12 or U13 levels, the most physically dominant player often gets cast as a central midfielder. But the 8.5 isn't about size — it's about spatial awareness, decision-making, and the ability to link phases of play. Prioritise cognitive sharpness over brute force. You can build an engine later. You can't bolt on football IQ.

The earlier you spot it, the earlier you can start building a development plan — one that doesn't force the player into a rigid role, but instead opens up a world of complexity.

Teaching Spatial Awareness

If there's anything that defines the elite 8.5s — the Gündogans, the Pedris, the De Bruynes (in his deeper iterations) — it's their preternatural awareness of space. They don't just find space. They shape it. They manipulate it.

You must teach your player to see the pitch not as zones but as dynamic layers. Static drills won't do it. You need to incorporate exercises that constantly shift spatial reference points. Think position-specific rondos, but with moving gates. Think five-a-side games where the pitch rotates 90 degrees every two minutes. Think transition games with variable overloads.

More importantly, train them in *"what ifs."* What if the winger tucks inside? What if the pivot is marked? What if the right-back inverts? Make your player an anticipator, not a reactor.

Interface this with video work. Show them patterns from elite midfielders: how they drift from the blind side of a marker, how they check their shoulder three times before receiving, how they alter their run to create a passing lane rather than sprint into it. Break it down frame by frame. Then replicate it on the pitch.

One of the most underused tools in youth development? Silent play. Run a portion of training where communication is non-verbal. Players must rely on body cues, scanning, and positional triggers. It forces your 8.5 to read the game visually, not just aurally — a huge advantage in noisy, chaotic match environments.

Encouraging Two-Footedness

If you want a player to operate in tight central corridors, under pressure, and in fluid rotations, they must be two-footed — not just for passing, but for balance, receiving, and shielding. This isn't a luxury. It's foundational.

Build this daily. Every technical drill should be mirrored: left foot, right foot, alternate foot. But also layer this into tactical setups. For example, in exercises where the 8.5 has to receive on the half-turn, force them to open up with their weak foot. In tight rondos, only allow passes with the non-dominant foot. In small-sided games, count double for goals or assists made with the weaker side.

And don't stop at passing. Encourage weak-footed ball-carrying. Ask them to shield with the opposite foot under pressure. Build confidence in using their entire body, not just their dominant side.

You're not aiming for perfection. You're aiming for unpredictability. A two-footed 8.5 can pivot in any direction, escape pressure with either foot, and disguise intentions far better than the one-footed wunderkind who eventually gets sussed out at senior level.

Finally, reward it. Analyse game film with your player and highlight instances where their weak foot unlocked a passing lane or helped them beat a press. Reinforce the value. Let them see what you see.

This is the foundation. You're not creating a midfielder. You're cultivating a football brain wired for ambiguity, movement, and control. A player who doesn't fit neatly into a formation board — but one who makes every formation work a little better. That's the 8.5. And it starts here.

Training Methodologies

If you want to develop an elite 8.5, your training sessions need to be surgical. Not generic. Not just high-intensity for the sake of it. Precision training tailored to the hybrid demands of this role. The 8.5 doesn't just run hard—they think faster, move smarter, and shape the geometry of the game. That doesn't come from running laps. It comes from designing environments where decision-making is constant, technical actions are repeated under cognitive stress, and transitional moments are baked into the DNA of every drill.

Let's break down how to build those environments.

Small-Sided Situational Drills

The traditional rondo is great—don't throw it out—but it's not enough. You need drills that replicate the chaos and micro-decisions of the match. Think 5v5s with conditions. Think 7v4 overloads with a time constraint. Think 4v4+3 where the neutrals are required to play one-touch. The goal? Replicate the grey zones in a match where the 8.5 thrives.

Set up a 6v6 with channels and a mandatory bounce pass through a central neutral. Suddenly, your hybrid midfielder has to navigate between lines, offer angles, scan continuously, and make high-stakes decisions with minimal space and time. The drill becomes a neurological workout as much as a physical one.

Constraint-based design is your friend. Want to train third-man runs? Limit direct passes into the final third unless there's a wall pass or lay-off involved. Want to build pressing resistance? Use a 4v2 keep-away game, but with one pressing player allowed to recover after a pass—the 8.5 now has to recognise when to release the ball before the pressure arrives and when to manipulate the press into overcommitting.

Introduce chaos purposefully. Start with a structured pattern, then randomly insert an extra defender or allow only two touches for 20 seconds. The brain adapts through stress, and your 8.5 must learn to thrive in that stress.

A hybrid midfielder is not produced through endless repetition of isolated drills. They're built in game-representative environments where their every decision has a cost.

Position-Specific Video Analysis

You can't improve what you can't see. Video isn't a luxury— it's a necessity. But not all video analysis is created equal. For the hybrid midfielder, you need to zoom into the moments that most people skip over. Not goals. Not assists. The 5 seconds before and after a regain. The three subtle steps when shifting with a back four. The body orientation when receiving under pressure just inside the half-space.

Break down footage into recurring game states: **build-up, progression, counter-press, recovery**. In each segment, isolate your 8.5's positioning, scanning habits, first-touch choices, and movement in relation to teammates. Show them the difference between being available and being effective. *Availability* is standing in space. *Effectiveness* is standing where you'll draw a defender, create a passing angle, or open a line.

Overlay freeze-frames with simple annotations. *"Open body = three options."* *"Poor scan = blind to press."* *"Delayed support = full-back isolated."* You're not just showing mistakes—you're teaching pattern recognition.

Go beyond individual clips. Compile sequences. Show how one decision in the 30th minute created a knock-on effect in the 32nd. Show them how their movement off the ball triggered

106

a rotation that led to a goal. The 8.5 needs to understand their role in the ecosystem. When they see the cause and effect, they start playing with intention.

And don't just analyse matches. Record training drills, especially small-sided games. Show them how their habits under pressure in training mirror—or betray—their match-day performances. You want to close the gap between training behaviours and competitive execution.

Make video analysis a habit, not a punishment. 20 minutes, twice a week, focused on micro-decisions. It's mental reps. And like anything else, consistency compounds.

Conditioning for Repeat Sprint Ability

It's not about who can run the fastest. It's about who can sprint hard, recover fast, and sprint again. The 8.5 isn't a marathon runner. They're a sprinter who never gets a full rest. That's where repeat sprint ability (RSA) comes in. And it has to be trained deliberately.

A typical match sees elite midfielders cover over 11km, with 1,000+ directional changes and up to 70 high-intensity actions. But the 8.5's sprinting isn't straight-line. It's curved, reactive, multidirectional—and it often ends with a technical action under fatigue. So your conditioning needs to mimic that.

Forget isolated shuttle runs. Build your RSA into football-specific drills. Use wave patterns: 3v2 transition games where the recovering defender joins the next wave. Or timed passing drills where the 8.5 must make three support runs in 20 seconds across different zones. Each sprint is followed by a technical or tactical decision: **pass, press, scan, recover**.

Another method: split-pitch circuits. Divide the pitch into thirds. In the defensive third, they press and recover. In the middle third, they link play. In the final third, they make a late box run. Then jog back and repeat. Time it. Track their recovery. You'll start to see who has the engine to play the role and who needs work.

Monitor heart rate and lactate thresholds if you've got the resources. If not, use RPE (Rate of Perceived Exertion) and performance drop-off to gauge load. Push them to the edge of fatigue, then ask them to execute a pass under pressure. That's real conditioning. That's how you forge a midfielder who doesn't crumble in the 83rd minute when your team needs one more line-breaking run.

Recovery is just as critical. The best 8.5s know how to recover without disappearing. Teach active recovery: subtle positional adjustments that hide effort but maintain availability. One smart step can buy them five seconds of rest and keep the team ticking.

And don't ignore the gym. Strength training isn't about aesthetics—it's about robustness. The 8.5 gets clattered often. Build glute-ham strength, single-leg stability, and rotational core power. A strong base prevents injuries in high-collision zones.

Finally, integrate decision-making into fatigue. Don't wait until players are fresh to coach tactics. Teach them how to think when tired. That's when the poor decisions come. That's also when the match is won or lost.

An elite 8.5 doesn't just endure the game—they shape it under duress. So train them to be comfortable in the uncomfortable. Not just physically. Cognitively. Tactically. That's the difference.

Mindset and Mental Models

If you've ever watched a midfielder dominate a match without touching the ball every five seconds, you've seen the impact of mindset and mental models in action. These are the invisible levers that separate the good from the transcendent. No amount of technical polish can replace a brain that anticipates before others react. In the 8.5 role—where decisions unfold in milliseconds and space vanishes in the blink of an eye—mental sharpness isn't optional. It's foundational.

This isn't about motivational posters or empty clichés. This is about the cognitive scaffolding that allows the 8.5 to adapt, lead, and thrive in the chaos of modern football.

Let's unpack three pillars: **Leadership in midfield, Tactical Empathy**, and **Anticipation over Reaction.**

Cultivating Leadership in Midfield

Leadership in the 8.5 role is less about shouting orders and more about tempo control, decision influence, and game intelligence that radiates calm. Forget armbands. The hybrid midfielder leads by example. You set the rhythm with your movement. You stabilise the team with your positioning. You turn a two-second window into a five-second opportunity because your teammates trust your judgement.

This kind of leadership doesn't need a podium. It thrives in the current of the match.

Vocal vs. Non-Vocal Leadership

You don't need to be the loudest to be the clearest. In fact, many of the best 8.5s lead through non-verbal communication: a subtle gesture to shift shape, a glance to trigger a press, a pause that tells the pivot to rotate out. These are micro-leadership moments. A good 8.5 sees the connections between moments and players. A great one nudges them into alignment.

Whether you're 17 or 30, you don't wait for permission to lead in this role. You build credibility through consistency. That means showing up for the ugly minutes—the ones where the game is messy, the lines are broken, and someone needs to restore order.

Decision Ownership

The hybrid midfielder is a decision amplifier. When you make the right call, your team benefits geometrically. That means you need the psychological muscle to own the bad ones too. You will misjudge a press. You will mistime a run. But the 8.5 isn't paralysed by mistakes—they integrate them. The faster you learn, the more trust you earn.

High-level coaches notice this. They aren't looking for a perfect pass rate. They want players who demand the ball after giving it away. Who lead the press after missing a tackle. That's leadership in the marrow of the role.

Building Tactical Empathy

Tactical empathy is the ability to see the game through the eyes of every role on the pitch. It's what allows the 8.5 to thrive in systems that morph mid-match. You don't just understand your job—you internalise the pressures and responsibilities of your teammates. This isn't soft skill fluff. It's tactical gold.

Reading the Needs of the System

Let's say your team is building from the back. The centre-backs are split, the pivot is being marked out, and the full-backs are inverted but static. The right 8.5 doesn't wait for a coach to scream an adjustment. You drop into the half-space to create a triangle. You give the goalkeeper an angle. You become the solution.

That's tactical empathy in motion. You're not solving for yourself—you're solving for the system.

This becomes even more critical when your side is out of possession. The 8.5 sees the forward's body shape and presses accordingly. You sense when the winger needs cover, when the pivot is overloaded, and when to hold shape instead of chasing shadows. You aren't just executing tactics—you're translating them across roles in real time.

Training the Empathy Muscle

You build this capacity through exposure and reflection. Watch matches from different player perspectives. Not just the midfielders. Spend time analysing how the full-backs trigger movements, how the centre-backs step into midfield, how the striker presses. Then, in your own sessions, ask better questions: *What was the 6 trying to create when I moved? What did my movement offer the 10?* This is how empathy becomes predictive.

When you develop tactical empathy, you become the glue. Coaches stop seeing you as a role and start seeing you as a system balancer. This is how the 8.5 earns the right to float, to adapt, to lead without a fixed GPS tag.

Teaching Anticipation over Reaction

If football is a game of time and space, anticipation is the ability to own both. It's the difference between being reactive and being inevitable. The 8.5 doesn't wait to see a pattern—they sense it forming. You anticipate not just where the ball will go, but why.

This is the hardest skill to teach and the most valuable to possess.

Cognitive Reps Over Physical Reps

You can run sprints until your legs give out, but if your brain is always a beat late, you're not a real 8.5. Anticipation is trained through cognitive reps: watching game footage, pausing sequences, predicting options. Start by asking: *What's the opposition trying to bait us into? What's the third option my teammate has? Where is the space that doesn't exist yet?*

Players like Nicolo Barella and Sergej Milinković-Savić don't win games with pace—they win them with arrival. They read the cues: a defender's hips, a teammate's head turn, a midfielder's hesitation. They don't just predict—they position early to shape the next phase.

This is where anticipation becomes a platform for control. You dictate the tempo not by speeding up the game, but by being ready before anyone else knows what's next.

Drills That Train Pattern Recognition

You don't need a neuroscience lab to build anticipation. You need game-realistic drills that force you into decision loops. One-touch rondos with constraints. Reduced-space positional games where you must scan before receiving. Shadow play sequences where players rotate before the ball is played.

The key is to overload decision-making, not just touches. Force your brain to filter, predict, and act. Then slow it down with video. Review what you didn't see in real-time. Over weeks, your anticipation sharpens. You stop reacting to the game and start curating it.

The Confidence Loop

Here's an edge most players ignore: *anticipation breeds confidence,* and *confidence accelerates anticipation.* When you trust your reads, you commit earlier. When you commit earlier, you influence outcomes. This loop is where elite 8.5s live.

But it's fragile. One poor decision can trigger doubt, and that doubt slows everything. Which is why mental recovery is part of the model. You learn to reset fast. You dissect errors clinically, not emotionally. You ask: *Was my read wrong, or was the timing off?* This clarity is what keeps your anticipation engine running clean.

The 8.5 role is designed for those who see football not just as a game of physicality, but as a dynamic puzzle. Leadership, empathy, and anticipation aren't abstract traits—they are functional assets. They let you operate in ambiguity and still bring clarity. They turn you into the player who doesn't just fit into systems—you elevate them.

And in the modern game, that's priceless.

9

Scouting the Future: Identifying Tomorrow's 8.5

Attributes to Monitor

Walk into any academy, scouting room, or YouTube rabbit hole of wonderkids, and you'll hear the same buzzwords ricocheting off the walls: *"versatile," "press-resistant," "reads the game well."* But when you're hunting for a future 8.5—the unicorn role of modern football—those descriptors barely scratch the surface.

You're not just looking for a player who can pass and press. You're looking for someone who can do both while decoding the game like a chess grandmaster, all in the blink of a second. This is the frontier of football intelligence—where raw tools meet pattern recognition, and role fluidity becomes an instinct, not a tactic.

Let's unpack the three attributes that matter most when scouting the next evolution of the all-phase midfielder.

Versatility in Phase Play

This isn't about being a jack-of-all-trades. It's about being a master of transitions.

You want to see how a player behaves when the game state flips. When their team wins the ball and immediately seeks to break lines. Or when they lose it and have to reconfigure their positioning in a heartbeat. The real 8.5 doesn't need a second invitation—they're already moving into the next phase.

Is the player comfortable in both slow, possession-heavy sequences and high-tempo, end-to-end chaos? Watch how they adapt. Do they play the same pass regardless of scenario, or do they adjust their tempo, body shape, and decision-making depending on what the game demands?

The tell isn't always in what they do—but in what they choose not to do.

A true 8.5 will sometimes delay a pass, not because they're uncertain, but because they're baiting the press to open a new lane. They might not charge forward immediately on a counter, instead ghosting into a secondary wave, arriving in the space vacated by defenders drawn to the initial break. That's phase literacy.

And this isn't just about transitions between attack and defence. It's transitions within possession: from build-up to progression, from progression to the final third. Watch how they move through these gears. Are they always in the right zone to offer *support, recycle,* or *probe?*

When assessing versatility in phase play, ask yourself:

· Does the player change their role dynamically within a single passage of play?

- Do they maintain positional discipline or freelance in ways that break team structure?
- Can they impact the match from multiple vertical and horizontal zones?

If the answer is yes to all three, you may be looking at someone who can operate as the fulcrum of modern fluidity.

Non-Verbal Communication with Teammates

It's easy to fall in love with a player's touch or their passing range. But the real gold is in what you don't hear.

Football is a game of signals—many of which don't come from shouting or arm-waving. The best 8.5s operate like human routers, constantly syncing with those around them through subtle cues: a head tilt, a scan just before moving, a micro-check of the shoulder before adjusting their run.

When you watch elite midfielders in real time, it's like watching high-level jazz musicians. They're improvising, yes, but off a shared sheet of music. The tempo, rhythm, and spacing all align because they're hyper-attuned to each other.

You need to look for players who communicate with their environment more than they do with their mouths. **This includes:**

- Checking over their shoulder multiple times before receiving.
- Adjusting their body shape to signal whether they want a ball to feet or into space.
- Using slight movements to drag markers, opening passing

lanes for others.

This kind of communication isn't taught in drills. It's cultivated through reps, awareness, and a high footballing IQ.

And it works both ways. Watch how teammates respond to the player. Do they trust them with the ball in tight areas? Do they make runs expecting the pass, even if it doesn't come every time? That trust is earned through a pattern of intelligent decision-making and non-verbal synergy.

If you're scouting live, sit in a spot where you can see the player's off-ball movement clearly. Spend entire passages of play watching them, not the ball. That's where the secrets live.

Adaptability to Multiple Formations

This one's the silent killer in most scouting reports. A player might look electric in a 4-3-3—pressing high, making late runs, spraying passes. But drop them into a 3-4-2-1 or a 4-2-3-1, and they become anonymous. That's not an athlete issue—it's a system fit problem.

To spot a true 8.5, you need to see how they function across tactical shapes. Not just where they line up, but how their responsibilities shift—and whether they rise or retreat in response.

Let's say a player shines in a single pivot system. Great. But can they also thrive in a double pivot, where their defensive responsibilities increase and their chances to drive forward may be limited? Or can they play as one of the two *"free 8s"* in a 3-2-5 structure, constantly rotating with wingers and full-backs?

Positional intelligence is about more than spatial awareness. It's about understanding role elasticity. When the formation shifts mid-game—say, to a back three in possession—does the player drop into the pivot to help build, or do they push higher to occupy the half-space? Do they instinctively take up new relationships on the pitch, or do they look lost in translation?

Scouting this requires watching multiple full matches, ideally across different competitions or tactical settings. **Look for:**

- Consistency in decision-making regardless of tactical system.
- The ability to find rhythm with new midfield partners.
- Awareness of space when structural references change.

The 8.5 isn't a plug-and-play role. It's a role that demands adaptation and interpretation. The best ones don't just survive in multiple systems—they translate their impact through them.

And here's where the role becomes self-selecting. Players who can't adapt to at least three different tactical shapes won't survive long at the elite level. The modern game is too fast, too fluid, too system-centric. This is no longer about fitting into a formation—it's about making the formation fit around the player's intelligence.

You know you're watching something special when a player doesn't just follow the play—they forecast it. They see not only where the ball is, but where it wants to go. They don't chase space—they shape it.

Scouting the 8.5 isn't about checking boxes. It's about identifying the players who warp the game by being one step ahead of it. They're not always the flashiest. They might not even play the final pass. But they're the ones who make the move possible.

And that's the player you want in your system. The one who doesn't need the spotlight—because they already understand the script.

Metrics that Matter

Numbers are your allies—if you know which ones to chase and which ones to ignore. The modern 8.5 doesn't live in the traditional stat sheet. You're not looking for goals and assists alone. You're tracking fingerprints on the strings of the game. Think of the 8.5 as the rhythm guitarist in a rock band—rarely in the spotlight, but holding the entire song together. So, how do you measure influence when it's subtle, layered, and often invisible to the naked eye?

Let's break down the performance indicators that cut through the noise and expose the DNA of a true hybrid midfielder.

Progressive Actions Per 90

If there's one number that acts like a seismograph for midfield dynamism, it's this. Progressive actions per 90 combines progressive passes and progressive carries—essentially any forward movement that breaks lines, forces defensive reshuffling, or tilts the pitch in your favour.

You want to know who's actually moving the ball with intent? Start here.

Progressive passes aren't just forward balls—they're contextually aggressive. They bypass multiple defenders, reach zones between the lines, and often lead to destabilised defensive shapes. Likewise, progressive carries measure how often a player moves the ball upfield with control, ideally through congested zones.

The 8.5 doesn't just circulate possession—they disrupt patterns. High progressive action stats suggest a player who isn't just participating but shaping the tempo and direction of the match. You're looking for midfielders with the courage to challenge the status quo of a game, not just play it safe.

Data providers like StatsBomb and Wyscout offer deeper layers—*progressive actions under pressure, progressive actions following a regain,* and even *progressive actions into the final third.* Those are gold mines for identifying an 8.5 who thrives in chaos and compression.

Pressure Regains in the Middle Third

This is where the 8.5 becomes more than a metronome. They become a hunter.

Pressure regains measure how often a player wins the ball back within five seconds of applying pressure. When narrowed to the middle third, this stat filters out high-pressing forwards and deep-lying destroyers, focusing instead on those who operate in the engine room.

The elite 8.5 doesn't just press—they press with purpose. They read triggers, close angles, and recover possession in moments that can swing momentum. If a player is consistently posting high pressure regains in midfield, they're not just chasing shadows—they're creating turnover opportunities that fuel transitions.

Why the middle third? Because that's the zone of maximum tactical tension. It's where build-ups are born and broken. A high volume of regains here suggests a player with both the anticipation and the physical engine to repeatedly disrupt and reset.

And here's the nuance—look at *"pressure regains leading to shots within 10 seconds."* That's the 8.5 with teeth.

Expected Threat (xT) Contribution

You've heard of xG. Maybe xA. But xT—Expected Threat—is the next frontier for evaluating true creative influence.

xT isn't about finishing. It's about movement and passing that increases the likelihood of a scoring opportunity. It tracks where the ball is moved from and to, and calculates how much more dangerous the latter location is. Think of it as a threat heatmap.

The 8.5 thrives on xT because their job isn't just to complete passes—it's to destabilise. A sideways pass from a pivot might have a low xT. But a vertical thread into the half-space, followed by a quick layoff to a winger in a 1v1? That's an xT spike.

You want to look at cumulative xT contribution—not just per pass, but over the course of a match or season. Who's adding value to every phase of possession? Who's consistently nudging the ball closer to danger zones, even if they're not delivering the final ball?

xT also rewards players who understand angles, timing, and movement. That's the essence of the 8.5. They don't just pass where the player is—they pass where the space is about to open.

Zone 14 Entries and Involvement

Zone 14—the strip of grass just outside the top of the penalty area, dead centre—is the most sacred real estate in football. It's the area where key passes happen, defensive lines collapse, and decision-making becomes a high-stakes game.

An effective 8.5 will show a high frequency of involvements in this zone—either receiving passes here, making passes from here, or moving into this area during attacking phases.

More nuanced data will show you how often the midfielder arrives in Zone 14 unmarked, how often they combine in tight triangles here, and how frequently their decisions in this zone lead to high xG chances.

Zone 14 data isn't just about who gets there—it's about how. You want players who arrive late, undetected, and with the awareness to exploit a fractured defensive shape. If the data shows repeated successful entries and impactful touches here, you're likely looking at an 8.5 who's mastered timing and positioning in attack.

Carries into the Final Third Under Pressure

Not all carries are created equal. Anyone can dribble in space. What separates the elite hybrids is their ability to carry the ball into dangerous areas while being harassed, pressed, and crowded.

This stat strips away the fluff. It isolates the players who can not only receive in tight areas, but turn, drive, and split lines under duress. It's especially valuable for 8.5s who operate in transitional systems—think of players who collect a second ball in midfield, ride a challenge, and immediately break into the final third.

You also want to look at the outcome of these carries. Do they lead to passes into the box? Shots? Fouls won in key areas? Carries under pressure that result in attacking sequences are a strong indicator of a player's resilience, decision-making, and spatial awareness.

This is one of those metrics that combines the physical and

the cerebral. It's not just about speed or strength. It's about knowing when to accelerate, when to shield, and when to release.

Progressive Passes Received

A subtle one—but telling.

This measures how often a player receives passes that break lines. It flips the script. Instead of looking at who initiates progression, you see who's trusted to be on the end of it.

A high number here suggests two key things: *spatial intelligence* and *trust.* Coaches and teammates believe this player knows how to find space, present the right body shape, and control difficult passes under pressure.

It also acts as a proxy for tactical positioning. 8.5s who consistently receive progressive passes are usually operating in pockets between lines—often in the half-space or just behind a pressing forward line.

You want to pair this with reception data—how cleanly the ball is controlled, what the next action is, and whether the player turns or plays back. A truly effective 8.5 not only receives progression—they amplify it.

Touches Per 90 in High-Impact Areas

Zone-based touches can reveal patterns that raw possession stats miss. You're interested in touches per 90 in three specific areas: *central midfield, the right and left half-spaces in the final third,* and *Zone 14.*

Why these? Because that's where the hybrid midfielder operates between roles. Too high a concentration in deep areas might suggest a player stuck in a build-up loop. Too far forward, and you're looking at a ten disguised as a hybrid.

Balanced, consistent touches across these zones indicate a player involved in all phases—someone who drops to assist the pivot, pushes into the final third, and connects wide rotations. This is your midfield glue.

Layer this with pass completion percentage in these zones and you'll get a read on technical consistency under pressure. The best hybrids aren't just active—they're efficient.

Receptions Between the Lines Per 90

This is where the magic lives. Receptions between the midfield and defensive lines show you who's brave enough to get in the mess and skilled enough to make it worthwhile.

The 8.5 thrives on these receptions—not static, standing in space—but on the move, at angles, with body orientation that opens multiple passing options. You want players who can receive on the half-turn, who understand when to show, and who constantly manipulate defenders with their positioning.

This is one of the most role-specific metrics for the hybrid midfielder. Players who rack up receptions between the lines at a high rate are usually the ones who make the subtle, invisible plays that unlock compact blocks.

Pair this with forward passes after reception and you've got a profile of a player who doesn't just receive in space—they exploit it.

Key Takeaways from the Metrics

You're not looking for unicorns who top every metric. You're assembling a mosaic. Some 8.5s lean more toward the creative, others toward the disruptor. What you want is a consistent pattern of influence across multiple phases of play.

Metrics matter when viewed in clusters. A midfielder with high progressive actions, strong pressure regains, and consistent Zone 14 involvement? That's a blueprint for a modern hybrid. One who's not just present—but pivotal.

Scouting in Context

When you're watching a player in action—especially one with the potential to become a top-level 8.5—you're not just watching them. You're watching the system. The context. The constraints. The ecosystem they're thriving in or being limited by. Talent doesn't exist in a vacuum, and neither does tactical intelligence. If you want to identify tomorrow's hybrid midfielders, forget highlight reels and raw stats. You need to understand how their current environment is shaping what you're seeing—and what it might be hiding.

Evaluating within Team Systems

No player performs in isolation. Every action, movement, and decision is a response to multiple inputs—team tactics, opposition structure, game state, coaching philosophy, and even pitch conditions. So when you're watching a potential 8.5, your first job is to reverse-engineer their ecosystem.

Start by asking: what system is this team playing, and what is this player being asked to do within it? A midfielder in a 4-3-3 might be tasked with progressive carries and late box entries, but in a 4-2-3-1, that same player could be operating closer to the forward line with more final-third creativity and less build-up involvement. The same player might look passive in one system and dynamic in another—because the instructions change, the spaces change, the responsibilities change.

If a player is in a double pivot, are they the more defensive sitter, or the one pushing into the half-spaces when the team has the ball? Are they initiating the press or covering passing lanes? These positional nuances matter because the 8.5 isn't defined by a fixed role. It's defined by adaptability and a high footballing IQ—the kind that reads the flow of the game and responds with the right action at the right time.

Also, look beyond the tactical board. Some players are being system-restricted. Coaches who don't trust youth, rigid tactical schemes, or teams playing to survive rather than dominate— these factors can all suppress a player's natural instinct. A midfielder might be capable of operating as an 8.5, but is being told to *"keep it simple,"* to *"protect the shape,"* or to *"leave the attacking third to the front four."*

What matters is this: can you spot the glimpses? The moments where they break the script and show initiative? A sharp third-man run in a stale system. A disguised pass that breaks a line even when their team is playing sideways. A subtle check into the blindside before receiving under pressure. These are your signals.

The next step is comparing their output against the team's structure. Are they outperforming their tactical constraints? Are they compensating for the weaknesses of others? For example, a midfielder who consistently drops into the full-back space to offer an outlet may be covering for a teammate who's positionally undisciplined. That's not just good positioning— it's tactical empathy.

And then there's the intangible: trust. How often do teammates give them the ball in tight areas? Do they become a reference point in transitions? Do they get the ball back after giving it? These patterns are often more revealing than pass completion rates. They show how the player is perceived within the system—whether they're a cog or a conductor.

Role Projection in Different Leagues

The qualities that define an elite 8.5 don't always translate cleanly across leagues. A player dominating in the Eredivisie or Liga NOS might look like a future Ballon d'Or candidate, but put them in the Bundesliga or Premier League and suddenly their time on the ball is halved and their passing lanes are tighter.

So when you're scouting, think beyond the current league. Ask yourself: how would this player's skillset translate if the tempo were higher, the duels more physical, and the spaces more compressed?

Start by analysing how the player handles pressure. In slower-paced leagues, players often have two or three touches to make a decision. In top-five leagues, it's sometimes one touch—or no touch at all. Does the player scan early? Can they play in one or two touches when pressed? Do they carry the ball into traffic intentionally to draw out defenders and then offload cleanly? These are all signs that they'll survive—and even thrive—in more intense environments.

Next, look at their off-ball movement in relation to space and timing. In leagues where teams defend deeper, players can get away with static positioning and still receive comfortably. But in high-pressing leagues, timing is everything. Does the player move into space before the ball is played or after? Do they anticipate where the second ball will land? Can they make supporting runs that create options without needing the ball?

Then consider the physicality. This doesn't just mean strength or tackling ability. It's about repeat sprints, recovery runs, the ability to stay balanced under contact, and the stamina to impact both ends of the pitch over 90 minutes. The 8.5 is a dual-threat position—it requires a player to be involved in first-phase build-up and also arrive in the box for a cutback. Not every league demands this. But the elite ones do.

Finally, assess the league's tactical culture. Serie A, for instance, is more structured and defensively disciplined, which can be a great testing ground for a player's positional awareness and spatial discipline. La Liga emphasises technical security and combination play. The Premier League demands physical robustness and verticality. Each league creates a different lens through which to evaluate potential.

So when you see a player dictating tempo in Austria or Norway, ask yourself: are they doing this because they're special, or because the context allows it? And then flip it: if you dropped them into a more complex tactical system, would their decision-making still hold up?

Tracking Developmental Trajectory

Talent is potential—but without progress, it's wasted.

To scout an 8.5 effectively, you need to track where they've been, where they are, and where they're heading. This is where you move from snapshot scouting into longitudinal evaluation.

Start with their positional history. Has the player always been a midfielder, or did they come through as a winger, full-back, or even a centre-back? Many of the best hybrid midfielders didn't start there. Some were attackers who learned to drop deep and connect play. Others were defenders who developed the confidence to step forward with the ball. The more varied the player's background, the more likely they are to have a broad understanding of spatial relationships—and that's gold for an 8.5.

Then look at usage over time. How has their role changed across seasons? Across managers? Across different game states? A player who can shift from a pressing eight to a deep-lying playmaker, or from a wide shuttler to an interior connector, is showing the kind of flexibility that modern systems crave. But more importantly, they're showing growth.

Monitor the complexity of tasks they're being given. Are they being trusted with set-piece routines, tempo control, and communication responsibilities? Are they being played in multiple positions over a season? Are they captaining youth sides or acting as on-field organisers? These are signs that the coaching staff sees more than just technical ability—they see leadership, intelligence, and system understanding.

Injury history matters too. Not just the injuries themselves, but how the player responds. Did they come back sharper? Slower? More cautious? Did they evolve their game to compensate for physical limitations? Resilience isn't just about coming back—it's about adapting in the process.

Finally, track their decision-making evolution. This can be subtle. For instance, are they choosing to play forward more often over time? Are they scanning earlier? Are they making more off-the-ball runs instead of always demanding feet? These micro-adjustments are often the result of learning—

whether through coaching, film study, or just experience.

The key is to follow the curve. If a player is stagnating in a lower league with little improvement over 18 months, that's a red flag. But if they're refining their game, expanding their toolkit, and becoming more influential tactically—then you're watching someone on the ascent.

You're not just scouting what a player is. You're scouting who they're becoming. And for the 8.5—the most elastic, intelligence-driven role in modern football—that trajectory is everything.

10

Analysing the Role: Reading Matches Through the 8.5 Lens

Visual Cues in Live Matches

There's a moment—usually around the 17th minute of any high-level match—when the patterns start to unfold. The surface chaos of pressing, possession, and positional exchanges gives way to something deeper: structure hidden in motion. And right in the middle of it all, somewhere in the blur of midfield traffic, is your 8.5. Not quite a classic playmaker, not strictly a box-to-box runner—something in between. Something essential.

To decode the 8.5 in real time, live from the touchline or the stands—or even your couch—you need to train your eye differently. While most spectators follow the ball, or perhaps the high-profile winger darting down the flank, you need to shift your gaze just a few degrees inward. That's where the real action is.

Body Orientation and Scanning

You can learn a lot from how a player stands. Not in isolation, but in context. Is their body half-turned to receive a pass from the pivot? Are they already glancing over their shoulder before the ball arrives? These habits aren't incidental. They're the habits of a player who lives ahead of the play.

The elite 8.5 scans constantly. They scan before receiving, after releasing, and even during transitions when the ball is nowhere near. It's not just head-turning for the sake of looking busy. It's targeted information gathering: where are the nearest opponents? What lanes are open? Where's the full-back—inside or overlapping?

You'll notice the best 8.5s rarely receive with their back to goal. Even in tight quarters, they find angles that allow them to play forward or sideways in one or two touches. Their hips are open to both the ball and the pitch. That body shape is the foundation of everything—because it allows them to play in 360 degrees, not just the narrow corridor ahead.

If you watch players like Pedri or İlkay Gündoğan in real time, you'll see this subtle choreography. They're never static. They adjust their angles constantly, almost like a satellite dish fine-tuning for signal strength. The pass doesn't have to be perfect, because they've already made the reception simple.

For coaches, this is gold. When watching your team—or your opponent—track how often midfielders receive on the half-turn. Are they scanning? Are they adjusting their feet and hips before the ball comes? If not, they're playing the game a step behind.

Movement Off the Ball

Forget the ball for a minute. Literally. Just don't watch it. Follow your 8.5 instead. Where are they going when the ball is with the centre-backs? Are they dropping into space between the pivots? Are they drifting wide to pull a marker out of the half-space?

The 8.5 doesn't just operate between the lines—they manipulate them. Movement off the ball is their silent weapon. They don't need to touch the ball to change the geometry of a possession sequence. Sometimes, by dragging a marker five yards to the left, they open a lane for a more direct pass to the striker. Other times, they ghost into space vacated by a decoy run, arriving unmarked just as the ball is recycled.

These movements are rarely random. They're responses to pressure, positioning, and teammates' cues. Watch Kevin De Bruyne. He'll shift wide only if the right-back tucks in. He'll make a run into the box only after the winger has engaged the full-back. It's a chain reaction, not a solo act.

When watching live, look for these triggers. Did the 8.5 drop when the opposition pressed high? Did they sprint into the box when the winger cut inside? Did they rotate positions with a forward to mask a defensive transition? When those movements become patterns, you've found your tactical fulcrum.

It's also worth noting the difference between active and passive movement. Is your 8.5 running to receive—or running to open space for someone else? Both are valuable, but the latter is often underappreciated. Coaches: reward unselfish movement in your analysis sessions. Players: study how top midfielders move when the camera isn't on them.

Positioning Between Opposition Lines

The phrase *"between the lines"* gets thrown around a lot. But in the context of the 8.5, it's not just positional—it's philosophical. This role thrives in ambiguity. They live in the void between the opponent's midfield and defence, constantly asking the back line a question: *step forward and risk space behind, or hold and let me receive?*

The best 8.5s don't just stand in this pocket—they pulse through it. They don't camp out; they arrive just in time. Timing is everything. Too early, and they attract a marker. Too late, and the passing lane is gone. **It's a dance with space and time.**

Watch how someone like Jude Bellingham positions himself when Madrid are building from the back. He doesn't always show for the ball. Sometimes he stays hidden behind the defensive midfielder, waiting for a slight shift before darting into view. That sudden availability is devastating. One vertical pass and he's facing the back line with options.

This positioning is also defensive insurance. If the 8.5 receives between lines and loses it, the team is exposed. So they're often positioned to either play forward or recycle quickly. Watch their first touch—does it go forward? Does it draw in a defender and create a new angle? If you're seeing square passes under no pressure, that's not a true 8.5 at work. That's a placeholder.

In live matches, try this: draw an invisible box between the opposition's midfield and defence. Now track how often your 8.5 enters it. How long do they stay? Do they receive and turn, or do they bounce it back first-time? That five-yard window is where the match often turns.

And then there's the defensive side. When your team loses the ball, what does the 8.5 do? Do they immediately press the ball carrier? Do they block the passing lane into the striker? Do they delay the counter long enough for the team to reset? Their positioning post-possession is just as critical as what they do on the ball.

This dual role—playmaker and presser—is what makes the 8.5 so tactically rich. It's not enough to float between lines. You have to control them.

—

If you're analysing a match from the stands, bring binoculars. Not for the long balls—but for the details. The feet, the hips, the head turns. If you're doing it from the bench, assign an assistant to focus only on your hybrid midfielder. Track their touches, yes—but also their influence in moments without the ball. And if you're watching on TV, ignore the commentary. Most pundits are still hung up on assists and shot volume.

The 8.5 isn't always the most visible player. But once your eye is trained, you'll see their fingerprints on everything. They're the invisible hand shaping the tempo, the space, the rhythm. And once you start watching matches through this lens, you won't want to watch any other way.

Breaking Down Video

The game isn't just played on the pitch—it's dissected in the film room. If you're serious about mastering or coaching the 8.5 role, you're not just watching highlights and goal compilations. You're rewinding sequences ten times. You're pausing on a midfielder's head swivel. You're noting the timing of a decoy run that never shows up on the stat sheet.

Video analysis is the microscope through which you can study the most underrated and misunderstood role in modern football. It's the forensic lab where intent, intelligence and instinct get translated into teachable principles.

Let's dive into how you can use video to decode the behaviours, decisions, and patterns of a true 8.5.

Identifying Role Responsibilities

The first step is clarity. What is the 8.5 expected to do in a specific system? Because without context, you're just watching a blur of movement. The hybrid role is chameleonic by nature—it adapts to the demands of the formation, the opponent, and the game state.

Start by defining the structural expectations. Is the player operating as part of a box midfield in a 3-2-5 structure? Are they the advanced midfielder in a 4-3-3, tasked with creating overloads in the half-space? Or are they a false 10 in a 4-2-3-1, floating between the lines to destabilise the opposition's midfield block?

Once you know the shape, start tracking the player's heat map—not just literally, but in terms of responsibility. Are they consistently showing for the ball in central zones? Are they the third man in wide triangles? Are they switching roles with the pivot or full-back?

One of the most revealing things you can do is chart their involvement in possession chains. Don't just look at touches. Look at touches with consequence. If you pause the video five seconds before a shot or a switch of play, how often is the 8.5

involved in the prelude?

This is how you distinguish between midfielders who are merely present and those who orchestrate.

Analysing Decision Trees

Let's talk about choice. Because the 8.5 lives in a world of options. At any given moment, they're balancing space, pressure, positioning of teammates, and the defensive shape of the opponent. Their value often lies not just in what they do—but in what they don't do.

To read their decision tree, slow the footage down. Literally. Use quarter or half-speed to isolate what the player sees. When they receive the ball, how many scans do they make beforehand? What's their body orientation telling you about their intentions?

Then map the options available:

 · Short pass to pivot
 · Diagonal ball to full-back
 · Carry forward into space
 · Quick wall pass with forward
 · Switch to opposite flank

Now track the choice made. Was it the optimal one? More importantly, was it the one that maintained tempo and disorganised the opposition? The best 8.5s aren't always flashy. They're tempo regulators. They make passes that unbalance defensive shapes without needing to play Hollywood balls.

Another layer: Look for delay or indecision. If the player hesitates, why? Was the passing lane closed? Was the movement ahead of them static? Was the timing off? These micro-moments reveal a player's processing speed and tactical clarity.

You'll also want to assess their decision-making during transitions. Watch how they react after a turnover. Do they instantly scan for counter-pressing cues? Do they drop into a defensive shape or gamble on a forward run? These choices are system-defining.

This kind of analysis doesn't just improve your understanding of the player—it sharpens your eye for tactical mechanics. You begin to see that every choice is a ripple in the system.

Understanding System-Specific Actions

Here's where it gets nuanced. The same action can mean different things in different systems. A third-man run in a Guardiola side has a different timing and purpose than one in a Slot setup. So when you're watching video, you need to decode behaviours in context.

Let's say you're watching a hybrid 8.5 in a 3-2-5 build-up. Their default position may be high in the right half-space. But what happens when the ball is on the left? Do they hold shape to create width for the switch? Or do they underlap into central zones to invite the inverted full-back forward?

Watch how they interact with their nearest team-mates. Are they synchronised with the winger's movements? Do they drop to form a double pivot when the opposition presses high? Do they rotate with the forward to create overloads?

System-specific actions are choreographed patterns. You'll start to notice that the best 8.5s don't just move—they trigger movement in others. When they drop, the winger adjusts. When they push forward, the pivot slides to cover. It's like watching jazz improvisation inside a classical framework.

Another key: defensive positioning. In systems that rely on pressing traps, the 8.5 might be tasked with shadowing the opposition's deepest midfielder. In others, they may float between lanes to cut off passing options. Watch for how they adjust their body shape to close angles, not just chase the ball.

The deeper you analyse, the more you'll start to see the fingerprints of the coaching philosophy. An 8.5 in a De Zerbi team looks different to one under Luis Enrique. Not because the player changes—but because the system demands different expressions of the same principles.

And that's the gold standard for video analysis: seeing the role through the lens of system logic. You're not just evaluating a player—you're reverse-engineering the tactical blueprint.

If you're reading this with the mindset of a player, you now have a framework to study your own game. If you're a coach, you've got a structure for feedback sessions that move beyond *"good pass"* or *"bad decision."* And if you're an analyst or scout, this is how you separate the system-reliant from the system-enhancing.

The 8.5 isn't just a role. It's a tactical hinge. And video is how you see the hinges operate in real time—quietly, intelligently, relentlessly.

Commentary & Narrative

There's a phrase that gets thrown around far too casually during live broadcasts: *"He's just drifting around the pitch."* It's often said with a tone of criticism, as if the player in question is

139

lost, unsure, or out of position. But if you're watching through the correct lens — the 8.5 lens — that same player might be orchestrating the match without ever touching the ball.

This section is for those of you who have grown tired of surface-level commentary. If you've ever shouted at your screen because the pundit missed a subtle press trigger, or because the co-commentator couldn't identify the third-man pattern unfolding right in front of them, you're in the right place. Understanding the 8.5 role demands more than identifying who scored or assisted. It requires reframing how we interpret the game, and more importantly, how we talk about it.

Let's pull back the curtain on a role that's too often invisible to the untrained eye — not because it doesn't exist, but because the language we use to describe football hasn't caught up with the evolution of the game.

How Pundits Miss the Hybrid Role

You've heard it a thousand times: *"He's playing as a number 10,"* or *"He's sitting deep like a traditional 6."* These are labels from a past era — shorthand used by pundits to simplify what they're seeing. But simplicity, in this case, equates to misdiagnosis. The modern midfield isn't built on rigid numbers. It's built on fluidity, context, and interdependence.

When a commentator says, *"He's not getting involved,"* what they might be missing is the player's role in unbalancing the opposition's shape. Gündoğan is the gold standard of this, hence the recurrent mention. He isn't always the most obvious figure on the pitch, but his off-ball movement creates overloads, disrupts defensive lines, and opens spaces for wide players to penetrate. That's not inactivity — that's orchestration.

The issue isn't just terminology. It's a lack of tactical literacy in mainstream punditry. The 8.5 thrives in ambiguity. He's not the deepest midfielder, nor the most advanced. He's not always the one making the final pass, nor the one recovering possession. But he's often the one who connects the moment before the moment — the pre-assist, the decoy sprint, the subtle rotation with a full-back that unlocks a new passing lane.

The traditional commentary framework doesn't have language for this. You'll hear *"good engine"* or *"hard-working midfielder,"* but you won't hear *"he manipulated the opposition's pivot by positioning himself a step wide of the half-space."* And yet, that's exactly what's happening.

If you're a coach or analyst, you already know the limitations of these narratives. They compress the game into soundbites, stripping nuance in favour of clarity. But clarity without context is misleading. And the 8.5 suffers most because his/her brilliance often unfolds in the margins — between the lines, between the phases, and between the minds of opponents.

Reframing Traditional Analysis

The vocabulary of football needs an upgrade. Not just to sound smarter, but to be more accurate. When you watch a match with the 8.5 in mind, you're not just looking for goals or assists — you're tracing influence. You're watching for how the game breathes through the middle third, and how space is manipulated without the ball.

Here's a practical shift: stop asking *"What did he do?"* and start asking *"What did he change?"*

Consider a sequence where the 8.5 drifts into the left half-space, takes one defender with him, and suddenly the winger has 1v1 space. He didn't touch the ball, but he changed the geometry of the attack. That's influence.

The 8.5 is the player who prompts rotation without gesturing. He drops slightly deeper, the pivot steps up, the full-back narrows, and suddenly the opposition press is misaligned. It's not spectacular. It's system hacking.

Traditional analysis often misses this because it's built on visible events — *goals, tackles, key passes.* But football is a game of invisible levers. The 8.5 pulls those levers. Your job is to retrain your eye to see them.

One way to do this is to track sequences backwards. Instead of focusing on the final ball, trace the origin of the move. Who created the angle that allowed the pass? Who pulled the marker out of zone? Who reset the tempo to invite the press? More often than not, you'll find the fingerprints of the 8.5 there.

And don't fall into the trap of equating *"quiet game"* with *"ineffective game."* The 8.5 might have fewer touches than the pivot or the winger, but his impact is often measured in the decisions he influences rather than the actions he completes. That's a shift in analytical mindset — from event-based to effect-based.

The New Language of Midfield Play

If you want to understand the 8.5, you need to start speaking the language. That means developing a vocabulary that reflects their reality — not as a hybrid of two roles, but as a distinct identity within a fluid system.

Start with concepts like *"occupying the blindside," "manipulating the second line,"* or *"bridging vertical phases."* These aren't buzzwords. They're tactical markers that define how the 8.5 operates.

For example, when you hear that a player *"arrives late,"* what you're really seeing is timing that exploits defensive scanning habits. Defenders check their shoulder, see no danger, and then — too late — the 8.5 ghosts in. That's not luck. That's choreography.

Or take *"half-space occupation."* The term itself sounds academic, but it's deeply practical. The half-space is the pocket between the centre and the wing — a channel that unsettles defensive shape because it's unclear who should close it down. The 8.5 lives there. Not constantly, but rhythmically. He dips in and out like a boxer feinting with footwork, always asking questions of the defensive structure.

Then there's *"positional rotation."* Not just players swapping spots, but doing so with purpose. When the 8.5 rotates with a full-back, it doesn't just confuse markers — it resets the build-up shape. It alters the pressing reference for the opponent. It creates a new angle for vertical progression. That's not improvisation. That's system fluency.

As a coach, this vocabulary becomes your toolkit. You use it to guide players, to analyse matches, to communicate intent. As a player, it becomes your internal compass — a way to process the game in real time. And as an analyst, it's how you extract meaning from movement.

The challenge is that this language is still emerging. Most broadcasts won't reference *"third-man runs"* or *"staggered lines of engagement."* But that's your edge. By shifting the language, you shift the lens. And by shifting the lens, you begin to see the game in layers, not lines.

So when the commentator says, *"He's drifting,"* you'll know better. You'll know he's positioning himself one step behind the second line, ready to trigger a press, or to become the free man in the next phase. You'll know that what looks passive is often preparation. What seems aimless is often anticipation.

Football is changing. The language must evolve with it. The 8.5 isn't just a role — it's a new grammar of the game. And once you learn to speak it, you'll never watch football the same way again.

11

Systems Thinking: How the 8.5 Impacts Team Strategy

Offensive Structures

When you watch a match with a trained eye, the goals often look like the end result of a dance—a synchronised, layered build-up where every player's movement is part of a larger mechanism. But if you zoom in, there's almost always one figure knitting the threads together in real time: the hybrid midfielder. The 8.5. They're not just an advanced 8 or a deeper 10. They're the tactical hinge upon which offensive systems balance, pivot, and explode.

This role doesn't live in isolation. It thrives—and becomes indispensable—within the broader offensive structure of the team. It's not just where the player is on the pitch, but how they think, how they react to triggers, and how they manipulate the game state to elevate the system around them.

Let's break this down.

Creating Numerical Superiority

One of the most misunderstood aspects of modern football is the concept of numerical superiority. Fans often focus on individual brilliance or the final pass, but what consistently unbalances defences is an extra man in the right zone at the right time. The 8.5 is a master of this.

They drift—not aimlessly, but with intent—into pockets where they draw defenders out or overload a line. Whether it's creating a 3v2 on the flank with a roaming full-back and winger, or joining the pivot to build a temporary triangle under pressure, the 8.5 acts as a force multiplier. You're not just adding a number; you're adding a brain that reads the game a second faster than everyone else.

The best teams don't rely on fixed positions. They engineer overloads in zones. PSG's midfield under Luis Enrique, Arsenal under Arteta, and Guardiola's City have all deployed versions of the 8.5 to create these micro-dominances in the half-spaces and between the lines. Space is rarely static, and neither is superiority. It's created, destroyed, and recreated—often within seconds.

With the 8.5 in your structure, superiority becomes intentional rather than accidental. You're not hoping a winger wins a 1v1. You're building a system that ensures he doesn't have to.

Facilitating Positional Rotations

Modern football is a game of rotations. Static systems get dissected. Pressing traps are set for predictable movements. So how do you stay unpredictable? By rotating roles without losing structure.

This is where the 8.5 operates like a chess master. They don't just move; they trigger others to move. When they drop into the half-space, it's not a solo decision—it's a signal. The full-back tucks in. The winger stays high and wide. The pivot shifts to cover. And suddenly, a 4-3-3 morphs into a 3-2-5 without a substitution or a pause.

This is not shape-shifting for the sake of aesthetics. It's func- tional design. You're giving defenders new problems to solve every 10 seconds. Think of Kevin De Bruyne drifting wide right and Savinho coming inside. Or Joao Neves rotating with Achraf Hakimi and Désiré Doué to create a triangle that overwhelms the touchline. These aren't improvisations. They're premeditated, rehearsed, and executed with the 8.5 as the fulcrum.

There's a reason why these players often have the highest number of touches in the final third without being traditional playmakers. They're not just getting on the ball—they're shaping the geometry of the attack. You watch them live and you'll notice: their movement opens lanes that didn't exist a second ago.

And when the team loses the ball? Because the 8.5 has operated in synchrony with others, the structure for counter- pressing is already in place. That's the beauty of intelligent rotations—they don't just attack better, they defend smarter.

Supporting Width and Central Overloads

You'll hear it in every tactical meeting: *"Stretch the pitch."* But it's not just about having wide players. It's about how you use them, and how you make the opponent choose between protecting the centre or defending the flanks. This is where the 8.5 becomes your system's pressure point.

They act like a valve for both width and centrality. When the opposition blocks the middle, the 8.5 can drift wide and combine with full-backs and wingers, creating triangles that pin defenders back. When the back line overcompensates and stretches too wide, the 8.5 exploits the central vacuum, arriving late, unmarked, and with purpose.

You're essentially making defenders pick their poison. Block the middle, and we'll isolate you wide in a 3v2. Step out wide, and we'll cut you open centrally with a third-man run into the box. The 8.5 is the one offering both options in real-time.

What makes this role especially potent is how it interacts with inverted full-backs and inside forwards. Let's say your left winger tucks in—now your left full-back overlaps. The 8.5 sees this and adjusts, either by providing a vertical option inside or by sitting behind to recycle possession. This dynamic creates unpredictability. Your offensive patterns don't become formulaic—they evolve during the match.

A classic example is Ilkay Gündoğan during Manchester City's 2020–2021 title run. Not a classic 10, not a deep-lying 8. But positioned as an 8.5, he timed his entries into the box perfectly, often finishing moves he'd helped initiate 20 seconds earlier. He played between the lines but read the space like a forward. Off the ball, he created central overloads. On it, he facilitated width. That's duality in motion.

In practical coaching terms, this means designing drills that teach your 8.5 to read the full width of the pitch—not just their own corridor. It's about developing spatial awareness that scans 270 degrees, not 90. They need to know when to stretch and when to collapse space, when to support the wing and when to punch through the core.

You don't need ten different build-up patterns. You need one intelligent player who can adapt the pattern to what the defence gives you. That's what the 8.5 does.

By embedding the 8.5 into your offensive structure, you move from playing positions to playing roles—fluid, intelligent, and reactive. You're not just building a team that can hold the ball. You're building one that understands what to do with it, depending on where the space is, who's been pulled out, and what the opponent has yet to anticipate.

This isn't about being trendy. It's about being effective. The 8.5 gives you the kind of tactical elasticity that turns a good team into a problem no one wants to solve on a Saturday afternoon.

Defensive Cohesion

One of the most underappreciated features of the 8.5 is how they quietly stitch together the defensive spine of a team — not by brute force or crunching tackles, but through spatial intelligence, anticipation, and synchronisation with the entire structure. When the ball is lost, they're not just there to help recover it. They're the glue that keeps the team compact, balanced, and ready to exert control again.

The 8.5 isn't a destroyer in the classic sense. They're not Roy Keane snarling through the midfield. They're more like Sergio Busquets in disguise — minus the deep-lying role. They win space before they win the ball. And in the modern game, that's often even more valuable.

Compactness Between Lines

You've probably heard coaches scream it from the sidelines: *"Stay compact!"* It's a tactical mantra, but for many players, it's just white noise. The 8.5 doesn't just hear it — they embody it.

What makes this role fascinating is how it helps compress the pitch vertically and horizontally. When your team loses possession, the 8.5 should be one of the first players to react — not by chasing the ball immediately, but by collapsing space. They drop into the seams between the lines, often alongside or just ahead of the pivot, forming a temporary double-screen that blocks access to central zones.

Now, here's the nuance. It's not just about standing in the right place. It's about reading the cues — body shape of the opponent, trajectory of the pass, positioning of teammates — and adjusting your movement in real time. There's a system, yes, but there's also freedom to interpret.

Take Luka Modrić when Real Madrid transition into a mid-block. He doesn't charge into tackles. He tucks in just enough to shade the passing lane to the 10, while also being in reach of a second ball. That's defensive compression with intelligence — and it's where the 8.5 thrives.

Another key element is vertical discipline. If the back four holds a line 35 yards from goal, the midfield can't be floating 15 yards ahead. The 8.5 helps ensure that the space between defence and midfield — the *"red zone"* where creative players love to operate — remains suffocatingly tight.

This positioning also allows for quick pressure traps. If the ball is played into an attacker between the lines, the 8.5 is close enough to collapse in with a teammate, forcing a rushed pass or turnover. It's not about diving in. It's about being the second man in the duel — the one who finishes what the first presser starts.

Pressing Traps Triggered by the 8.5

High pressing gets the headlines. The front three swarming like hornets. The goalkeeper forced into bad decisions. But none of it works without the midfielders — especially the 8.5 — setting the bait.

Let's break this down. Pressing isn't just about chasing the ball. It's a coordinated hunt. Think of it as a chess game. Each movement is designed to provoke a response. The 8.5 is often the queen piece — versatile, mobile, and capable of shifting the whole board.

The most effective pressing traps are inside-out. You want to tempt the opponent to play into the centre before collapsing on them. And who better to trigger that than the 8.5, sitting just off the shoulder of the opposition pivot?

Here's what it looks like in action. The ball is with the opponent's centre-back. Your striker curves his run to block the pass wide. Your winger tucks in slightly to cut the switch. This funnels the ball towards the middle. The opposition midfielder receives it — and bang, the 8.5 steps in. Not always to win the ball directly, but to force an error, a rushed touch, a square pass under pressure.

Sometimes, the 8.5 is the trigger. Other times, they're the second wave. In both cases, they must be cued into the press with near-telepathic timing. If they jump too early, they get bypassed. Too late, and the opponent turns and escapes. It's an art form, not a sprint test.

And let's be clear — pressing isn't just about regaining the ball. It's about where you regain it. The 8.5 helps coordinate these traps in zones where the counter is immediately danger-ous. Winning the ball high up is only half the battle. Winning it in the right pocket — that's when you punish teams.

Midfield As the First Line of Defence

Forget the narrative that defending starts at the back. In the modern game, it starts in midfield — and often, it starts with the 8.5.

When your team is out of possession, your centre-backs should be the last people you're relying on. If they're constantly exposed, something's failed higher up. That's where the 8.5 comes in. They're the firewall.

Their job isn't to break up every attack. It's to prevent the attack from ever materialising. That means disrupting the opponent's structure before it becomes dangerous. Think of it like a boxer jabbing to keep distance — it's not the knockout punch, but it controls the rhythm.

In practice, this looks like subtle positioning to block the turn of a receiving midfielder. Or shifting a few yards to steer the opponent towards a less threatening area. It's not glamorous. You won't see it on highlight reels. But it's the stuff that wins matches.

The 8.5 also covers for structural imbalances. If your full-back is caught high upfield, the 8.5 might shuffle across to plug the gap temporarily. If your pivot gets dragged out of position by a decoy run, the 8.5 drops in to maintain the shape. It's a role that requires constant scanning, constant adjustment. You're never static. You're always solving problems.

And then there's the matter of tempo control. The best 8.5s know when to slow things down. Not every turnover needs to be a sprint to goal. Sometimes, the smart play is to win the foul, take the sting out of the game, and reset the block. That's game management — and it often lives in the midfield.

One of the most telling signs of a well-schooled 8.5? They rarely foul in bad areas. When they do commit, it's tactical. It's calculated. They understand risk zones. They understand when to stop play and when to let it flow.

There's a reason managers trust these players. They're the ones who get a tactical yellow card in the 74th minute and still finish the game without a second booking. That's control. That's discipline.

And it's why the 8.5 is so integral to the defensive identity of a team. They're not just filling gaps. They're shaping the entire resistance — through positioning, anticipation, and coordination with everyone else on the pitch.

This isn't about defending in the traditional sense. It's about creating a system where defending becomes a collective act — not a desperate one. The 8.5 is the intellectual centre of that collective. Not just the lungs, but the brain. And when they get it right, the whole team feels more stable. More compact. More in control.

Transition Phases

The 8.5 isn't just a role. It's a rhythm-maker. A tempo-setter. A code embedded in the transitions of modern football. It's where the game breathes—between chaos and control, between loss and recovery, between hesitation and acceleration. If you want to understand the pulse of a team, watch how the 8.5 behaves in transition. Not when the ball is tucked into possession, but when the structure is breaking, reshaping, reacting. That's where you'll find truth.

Counter-Pressing from Midfield

Let's start with what happens a split second after possession is lost. The traditional instinct might be to drop, regroup, defend the zone. But in today's game, especially in elite-level systems, that pause is a luxury. The 8.5 must become a predator in that moment. Not out of desperation, but by design.

Counter-pressing isn't just about aggressive running; it's about intelligent positioning before the turnover happens. You don't win the ball back by reacting—you win it back by anticipating.

The best 8.5s operate on a hair-trigger system calibrated by visual cues, body language, and passing lanes. They scan constantly, not just to receive, but to identify where the next three passes might go if possession flips.

When the ball is lost, the 8.5 becomes the first responder. Their angle of approach matters. Their body orientation matters. Their timing matters more than their tenacity. Go half a second too early and you're bypassed. Go too late and you're chasing shadows. When done right, the 8.5 doesn't just recover possession—they destabilise the opponent's transition before it begins.

Take Bernardo Silva during Manchester City's high-regain phases. Notice how he doesn't just sprint towards the ball—he arcs, he curves, he angles his run to close off two options at once. It's not about pressing the man. It's about pressing the mind. You're forcing indecision. You're making the forward pass unattractive. That's how you turn a reaction into a strategy.

And when the counter-press fails? The 8.5 has to reset fast. They don't sulk or jog back. They become the metronome in reverse—resetting defensive shape on the fly, pulling wide players into compact lines, temporarily covering for full-backs caught high. Their attention to detail in these moments sepa-rates elite from average.

Launching Fast Breaks

Then there's the opposite moment—the euphoric heartbeat after a regain. You've got the ball. The opposition is stretched. The pitch is open. Now what?

This is where the 8.5 becomes the architect of chaos.

Think of this phase as controlled anarchy. You don't want to just hoof it forward and hope. You want to exploit the disorganisation with purpose. The 8.5's job is not always to carry the ball themselves—it's to orchestrate the break. That might mean the first-time release into the channel. That might mean dragging a defender with a lateral run to open space centrally. That might mean holding the ball just long enough to bait pressure and then release a third-man runner into space.

It's the pause before the pass that matters. The hesitation that draws the line out. The disguise that hides the true intent. Watch someone like Jamal Musiala or Dominik Szoboszlai in these moments. They don't just sprint forward—they manipulate defenders with subtle body feints, with decoy

155

angles, with tempo shifts.

This is where your training in pattern recognition becomes priceless. Is the striker peeling wide? Is the winger checking in? Is the full-back overlapping or tucking in? The 8.5 has to compute these moving variables in microseconds and choose the optimal path. Not just the available pass—the pass that hurts.

And here's a nuance: the 8.5 often doesn't finish the break, they sustain it. The goal isn't always to score immediately—it's to turn the transition into a sustained attacking phase. You force a corner. You create a wide overload. You draw a foul in a dangerous area. That's the hidden value of the 8.5: they reshape the transition into territory.

You'll also see how the 8.5 links with the advanced 10 or a false nine in these moments. It's not a straight-line partnership. It's interdependent. As the ball moves forward, the 8.5 must continue their run—not always to receive, but to occupy, to distract, to pull markers. It's the run that opens the space for someone else. That's what separates role players from system players.

Dictating Tempo Post-Recovery

Once the chaos settles, and the ball is yours, the 8.5 becomes the conductor. Not necessarily the loudest player on the pitch, but the one dictating how the next 10 seconds unfold. *Do we go again? Do we slow it down? Do we lure the press?*

Tempo control isn't about jogging or sprinting—it's about intentionality. The 8.5 must sense the emotional and structural state of both teams. Did the opposition just commit numbers forward? Are they retreating in panic? Are your teammates in sync or scattered?

This is where experienced 8.5s shine—they feel the match. Luka Modrić in his prime was a master of this. After a regain, he might take three extra touches, pull the ball back, scan, and switch play. Not because he was being safe, but because he understood the moment wasn't ripe. He created pauses to allow his team to breathe and reorganise. Then, when the window opened, he accelerated the rhythm with one disguised pass that split two lines.

The 8.5 needs to have what some coaches call *"situational memory"*—an awareness of what just happened and what it means for what's next. Did your left-back just lose a duel and is now out of position? Then maybe don't play the risky switch to that side. Did your striker just press the centre-back and force a bad clearance? Then yes, now's the time to hit the half-space and go again.

And when your team is leading, and the clock is ticking, the 8.5 becomes the game manager. They draw fouls. They recycle possession. They demand the ball in tight areas to slow things down. They kill the rhythm without killing the intent.

This is the psychological side of tempo control. The 8.5 isn't just playing the ball—they're playing the narrative of the match. They decide whether the game is frantic or composed. Whether the opponent feels in control or disoriented. Whether the crowd is nervous or expectant.

And here's a subtlety: the best 8.5s know when not to touch the ball. Sometimes their off-ball movement is the difference-maker. By pulling a marker, they open a passing lane. By feinting one way, they create an overload the other. Tempo isn't just about what you do with the ball—it's about how you shape the options around it.

When you break it down, the transitional moments are where the 8.5 truly earns their reputation. Not because they're flashy. But because they're foundational. They're the ones who ensure that when the game breaks, it doesn't fall apart. It evolves. It bends. It flows.

You can coach pressing systems. You can drill counter-attacks. But you can't automate feel. The 8.5 lives in that uncoachable space—the grey zone where instinct meets insight, where movement meets meaning, where transitions become turning points. Watch closely. That's where the game is won.

12

The Future of the 8.5: Where the Game is Going

Tactical Innovation

Rise of Total Positional Fluidity

There's a phrase that's becoming increasingly common among top-level coaches when discussing positional play: *"The position is the starting point, not the destination."* That single sentence captures the trajectory of modern football and, more pertinently, the evolution of the 8.5 role.

The traditional blueprint of tactics with static roles and defined zones is being torn up in favour of total positional fluidity. The 8.5—already a hybrid—is now evolving into something more abstract: a role that isn't defined by where a player starts, but by how he moves and adapts to the game's rhythm. This isn't about rotations within a triangle. This is about dissolving the triangle altogether.

Let's take Pep Guardiola's Manchester City as a case study. In recent seasons, his use of *"inverted full-backs"* morphing into midfielders, and midfielders stepping into defensive lines, is not just tactical wizardry. It's a blueprint for fluidity. The 8.5 in this system must read not only their own line but three others—because at any moment, he might be the one stepping into the defensive line or arriving in the penalty box as the furthest forward. That's the ask now.

You've probably seen midfielders like Ilkay Gündoğan, Frenkie de Jong, or Florian Wirtz operate in these roles. They don't 'play' positions. They interpret space. These are players coached not just to execute a role, but to understand the entire ecosystem of the team. They're taught to scan not just for the ball, but for shape, flow, and density. And that's why the 8.5 is at the centre of the move towards total positional fluidity—because they already think in multiple layers.

This fluidity is also tactical insurance. When the opposition sets pressing traps, the 8.5's ability to shift vertically or laterally creates new exit routes. When the team is in possession, he can become an auxiliary winger, a third centre-back, or a decoy nine. You're no longer looking for players who can "fill in." You're looking for players who are the system.

This trend is being accelerated by the increasing use of false full-backs, double false nines, and even centre-backs who step into midfield and act as playmakers. In systems like this, the 8.5 is often the player who dictates the tempo without ever being in the same zone twice in a sequence. He's a ghost and a constant presence at the same time.

If you're a coach or analyst, the question to ask isn't *"Where should my midfielder be?"* but *"Where can he create the most disequilibrium?"* That's the currency now—unbalancing the opposition. And the 8.5 is the trader.

Use of AI in Role Refinement

The game is no longer just coached on the pitch; it's being coded in data labs. The use of Artificial Intelligence in refining roles—especially something as nuanced as the 8.5—is no longer a future possibility. It's already happening in elite environments.

Let's start with AI-driven video analysis. Clubs like Liverpool, Bayern Munich, and Real Sociedad are deploying machine learning models that track sequences involving the 8.5—how often he breaks lines, how frequently he's involved in third-man combinations, how well he times his support movements. But it doesn't stop at counting actions; it starts predicting them. The software recommends movement patterns based on opposition shape, historical success, and even pitch zones where the player is most effective.

This isn't just about compiling heat maps. It's about building decision trees. AI models are now being used to simulate decision-making under pressure. If the 8.5 receives in the left half-space and the passing lane to the striker is blocked, what's his optimal next move? The model learns from hundreds of hours of match footage and generates probable outcomes. Coaches can then use this to create scenario-based drills that are not just realistic, but statistically optimal.

And it's not limited to post-match review. Some clubs are now integrating real-time AI feedback during training sessions. Players wear GPS and biometric trackers, and the data is processed live. If the 8.5 is late arriving in support zones or isn't pressing aggressively enough, the system flags it within seconds. It's a live coaching assistant.

AI is also helping in role profiling. Scouts and analysts are no longer relying solely on the eye test. Algorithms scan thousands of data points across leagues to identify players with the movement patterns, decision-making profiles, and phase adaptability that mirror elite 8.5s. A 19-year-old midfielder in Uruguay might never make it into a traditional scout's shortlist—but AI-driven modelling could flag him as the next evolution of the role.

Of course, there's the human element that can't—and shouldn't—be replaced. But AI's greatest contribution may lie in what it reveals about the unseen. The 8.5's game is full of hidden triggers, off-ball cues, and micro-adjustments that don't show up in traditional stats. AI can detect them, quantify them, and—crucially—train them.

If you're working in a football environment and not at least dabbling in AI-assisted role analysis, you're already behind. The next wave of midfielders will be coached not just with cones and bibs, but with algorithms and predictive modelling. And the 8.5, with his all-phase responsibilities, is the perfect test case for this hybrid of coaching and coding.

New Formations Emerging

Formations are evolving not just in structure but in purpose. We've moved from thinking about systems in terms of symmetry—like the 4-3-3 or 4-2-3-1—to understanding them as dynamic frameworks for controlling zones. This shift is giving birth to new formations specifically designed to empower hybrid roles like the 8.5.

One of the most intriguing developments is the return of the WM shape—but in its 21st-century form, the A-M - check out my book on this if you're intrigued. In possession, you're seeing a 3-2-4-1 shape with one of the "2" midfielders acting as a floating 8.5. They're not fixed to the centre; instead, they slides into half-spaces, arrive at the top of the box, and even drift wide to overload. This shape isn't dead space—it's a living organism, and the 8.5 is the synapse.

Another emerging concept is the "2-3-2-3" in build-up. Used by teams like RB Leipzig, Atalanta and a number of Bundesliga 2 sides, this shape creates a central column of five players with the 8.5 as the pivot between progress and protection. The innovation here is not just in vertical stacking but in creating maximum flexibility for horizontal shifts. The 8.5 can push into the attacking third or drop beside the pivot without needing to ask permission from the formation.

There's also experimentation with asymmetrical systems— formations that have no mirror image. Think a 3-1-4-2 where the right-sided 8.5 plays higher, acting almost like a narrow winger, while the left-sided midfielder stays deeper to balance transitions. These systems stretch and compress in real-time, and the 8.5 is often the hinge point.

These aren't gimmicks. They're responses to the tactical arms race that's playing out in elite football. Pressing struc-tures are more coordinated than ever. Defensive blocks are tighter, more zonally aware. So formations must evolve to disrupt, to provoke, to create moments of chaos. And the 8.5 is uniquely positioned to do all three.

If you're designing a system or refining a tactical identity, your formation is only as good as your most adaptive player. The 8.5, with his multi-phase intelligence, becomes the cheat code. Build your shape around his capabilities—not the other way around.

As these new formations mature, the 8.5 will become not just a role, but a tactical philosophy. A way of playing. A way of thinking. A way of controlling the game without ever being fixed to its geography. The future of tactical innovation doesn't lie in rigid patterns—it lies in fluid intelligence. And the 8.5 is its embodiment.

Role Expansion

The 8.5 role isn't just evolving—it's multiplying. It's no longer about sitting between the 8 and the 10. That's yesterday's definition. Today, the hybrid midfielder is stepping beyond the midfield grid and stretching their influence into zones and duties traditionally reserved for other specialists. You're not just looking at a connector anymore; you're looking at a play-making destroyer, a wide overload architect, and, increasingly, the tactical heartbeat of the entire team.

Let's get into the three key directions this role is expanding into. These are the shifts that could fundamentally alter how teams are built, how matches are won, and how the modern game is understood.

The 8.5 as a Playmaking Destroyer

Once upon a time, you had the destroyer and you had the creator. Roy Keane snarled and snarled some more. Juan Román Riquelme floated in silk slippers. They lived on opposite ends of the midfield spectrum. But the 8.5 is now being asked to live in both worlds—simultaneously.

This isn't just about being 'box-to-box'. That term doesn't

carry the nuance anymore. This is about initiating the press, winning the duel, and then immediately dictating the next three passes. It's Patrick Vieira with a PhD in positional play. It's Pedri turning defence into launchpad. It's Jude Bellingham pressing like a six and finishing like a nine.

Coaches are no longer separating the grit from the grace. They want both in one body. That means players in this role are being trained to read triggers like a defensive midfielder—cutting out passing lanes, stepping into gaps, hounding second balls—but also to see the pitch like a regista. Once possession changes hands, the 8.5 doesn't just offload it to a more creative teammate. They are the creative teammate.

You'll see them snapping into tackles just outside their own box, only to glide forward within seconds, breaking lines with a disguised reverse pass or drawing fouls in advanced areas. Not simply a transitional midfielder; a transitional force.

It's no accident that the top clubs are valuing midfielders with aggressive defensive metrics and high progressive pass accuracy. The data teams are catching up to what the pitch has been whispering for a while: the 8.5 must destroy and design.

Influence on Wide and Central Channels

Here's where things start getting horizontal. Traditional midfield roles lived centrally. The 6 sat deep. The 10 played in pockets. The 8 ran the channels between them. But now, the hybrid 8.5 is being used to manipulate space across the entire width of the pitch—not just its spine.

In possession-heavy systems, coaches are pushing the 8.5 into wider positions—not to hug the touchline, but to create overloads. It's about dragging opposition markers out of shape. You'll often see an 8.5 receive in the half-space, pull a full-back with them, and open up the lane for a winger or overlapping full-back to exploit. This isn't about touching the ball 100 times. It's about moving like a chess piece that forces three others to shift.

Think of Bernardo Silva when Manchester City invert their full-backs. He doesn't just drift wide to receive; he drifts to confuse. He forces the opposition to pick their poison—hold your shape and let the winger go, or follow him and open the middle. The 8.5 becomes the decoy and the detonator all in one.

In more transitional teams, you'll see the 8.5 controlling the central channel during quick breaks. They're not just supporting the striker; they're often the first to arrive in the final third, ghosting into central spaces while defenders are still turning their hips. Unlike a classic 10, who receives in front of the back line, the 8.5 is arriving behind them.

Wide influence also means defending laterally. In pressing systems, the 8.5 is often tasked with shifting across to engage on the flanks, especially when the winger stays high and the full-back is caught upfield. You're seeing a role that blurs the lines between central midfielder, winger, and auxiliary full-back.

This is why the best 8.5s are spatially literate. They have to be. They need to understand how their movement affects the shape—not just of their own team, but of the opponent's. This is not a 'stay in your lane' position. It's a *'know every lane and when to enter it'* position.

Leadership from the Middle

Not all leadership wears the armband. In modern football, leadership is increasingly tactical. And the 8.5 is fast becoming the role through which teams are led—not just emotionally, but structurally.

Think about who sees the most. The goalkeeper has the angle, sure. Centre-backs can orchestrate the first line. But it's the hybrid midfielder who sees both ends. They're the midfielder who knows when the press is losing shape, when the winger is too high, when the pivot needs to drop. They are the node through which the tactical mood of the team flows.

Leadership in this context means knowing when to slow the game down—not just with the ball, but with positioning. It means recognising when your team's structure is stretched and filling the gap without being told. It also means directing others—pointing, shouting, correcting. You'll notice the best 8.5s are constantly talking. Not just to the ref. To everyone.

This kind of leadership is being coached now. Youth academies are embedding tactical communication into their midfield programmes. Players are taught to scan not just for the next pass but for the next problem. They're trained to be the solution—before the coach has to shout it. Coaches want 8.5s who can play and manage the game from within the game.

In elite teams, the 8.5 is often the player who carries the tactical briefing onto the pitch. They're the ones adjusting the press shape on the fly. They're the ones flipping between a midfield three and a box depending on the game state. When the manager talks about *"intelligent footballers,"* they're talking about this player.

Leadership from the middle also means being brave. Not just

in big games, but in chaotic ones. When the plan breaks down—and it always does—it's the 8.5 who feels the responsibility to stitch it back together. They're the ones who drop into the back line if needed, who sprint forward to close a second ball when everyone else is ball-watching. It's leadership by default. Because no one else is closer to the action.

This is why the 8.5 is becoming the most irreplaceable role on the pitch. You can swap strikers, you can rotate full-backs. But if your hybrid midfielder is off, the whole organism stutters. The tempo drops. The angles disappear. The game becomes reactive, not proactive.

So, what does this mean for you? If you're a coach, you need to start identifying this leadership profile early. If you're a player, understand that your ability to lead tactically could be the difference between being a squad option and being undroppable. If you're an analyst or scout, look beyond the armband. Watch who's pulling the strings when the ball isn't near them. That's your 8.5.

This role expansion isn't theoretical. It's happening weekly in top leagues and trickling down rapidly. The hybrid midfielder is no longer a niche option—it's becoming the prototype. The 8.5 isn't just a connector anymore. It's the fulcrum, the amplifier, the architect, and increasingly, the captain you didn't know you had.

Development Pathways

If you want to future-proof your midfield, you need to start thinking well beyond the standard drills and coaching badges. The 8.5 isn't a role you stumble into anymore—it's a role you craft, layer by layer, rep by rep, decision by decision. This is about creating a complete footballer who can operate across the full bandwidth of the pitch and the full spectrum of tactical scenarios. And that starts with how players are developed, trained, and challenged from the very beginning.

Cross-Training in Multiple Roles

You can't build a hybrid if you only ever train a specialist. The true 8.5 isn't a Number 8 with a bit of flair or a Number 10 who occasionally tracks back. They're a fully integrated operator—part controller, part creator, part destroyer. And you don't get there by locking them into one channel of experience.

Cross-training is the fast lane to modern football literacy. That means exposing players to multiple roles across midfield: the single pivot, the double pivot, the attacking midfielder floating off the striker, even wide positions cutting inside. Each of these roles sharpens a different tactical blade. The pivot teaches tempo control and defensive awareness. The 10 role forces you to see gaps before they open. Shuttling as an interior wide midfielder gives you a feel for wing rotations and pressing traps.

In elite academies, the standout prospects aren't just the fittest or most technical—they're the ones who adapt. You'll see a 16-year-old playing as a left-sided 8 one week, then dropping as a false full-back the next. Not because they're being shuffled around, but because coaches are deliberately building a multidimensional game intelligence. That's cross-training done right.

You want a midfielder who can shift into a back three during build-up and still arrive late in the box fifteen seconds later. That doesn't happen unless they've lived those other roles. Cross-training isn't about positional flexibility for its own sake—it's about expanding the player's tactical vocabulary. The more positions you understand, the better you anticipate, support, and manipulate space.

And this isn't just for kids. Senior pros who want to evolve into a hybrid need to deliberately rewire their habits. Get out of your comfort zone in training. Play short-sided games in unfamiliar roles. Study teammates who excel in other positions. Every new lens adds another layer to your footballing brain.

Integrating Analytics into Coaching

Instinct still rules the game, but data is now your co-pilot. The elite 8.5s of the next generation won't just be scouted with analytics—they'll be developed using them. And not just raw numbers, but actionable, contextual insights that can shape how a player trains, recovers, and evolves.

Coaching with analytics doesn't mean turning training into a spreadsheet. It means using data to highlight patterns players can actually feel and act upon. Like showing a young midfielder how often they receive the ball facing their own goal versus facing forward. Or tracking their scanning frequency before receiving under pressure. These aren't abstract metrics—they're real behaviours that define effectiveness in congested zones.

Training sessions are becoming more feedback-rich. Wearable tech can now capture accelerations, decelerations, heart rate variability, and GPS heat maps in real time. Coaches can overlay this with video to show players how their physical output matches their tactical decisions. It's not just *"run more"*—it's *"see how your sprint pulled their pivot out of position?"* Now we're talking about intelligent intensity.

You've also got machine learning models that can suggest optimal pass choices based on historical patterns. More advanced setups use xT (expected threat) to evaluate not just whether you made a pass, but how much danger it created. And when players start to internalise that kind of feedback, their decision-making sharpens. They start seeing the game in layers—not just where the ball is, but what it could become.

But here's the key: analytics need translation. A coach has to bridge the gap between the numbers and the pitch. It's not enough to tell someone they're completing 87% of their passes. *Where? Under what pressure? In what zones? Against what shape?* The best coaches are becoming data interpreters—turning analytics into actionable coaching language.

This also changes how roles are taught. You can now build a development profile based on statistical archetypes. Want to build a Bellingham-style 8.5? Start by tracking progressive carries, pressure regains, and touches in the final third. Then design drills that replicate those actions under match conditions. You're not training in the dark anymore—you're reverse-engineering the role with precision.

And for the players? The ones who embrace this are the ones who climb. They learn to self-audit. They study their own data like a trader watches market trends. Not obsessively, but intentionally. The future 8.5s will be tacticians with boots on, using data not just to know where they've been—but to decide where they're going.

Building the Modern All-Phase Midfielder

You can't hide in modern midfield. The days of being *"just a deep-lying playmaker"* or *"just a final third operator"* are over. The 8.5 demands presence in all three phases of play—*build-up, progression*, and *final third execution.* That's what separates the good from the elite. And building that kind of player requires a total shift in how we think about development.

First, you have to train for tempo diversity. Most midfielders are good at one gear. They either play too slow or too fast. The modern 8.5 has to be a tempo architect—able to kill the game with a pause, then accelerate with one touch. That starts with session design: drills that force decision-making at multiple speeds. Not just rondos, but asymmetric rondos where the pressing team is overloaded, forcing faster reads. Or positional games where the player has to switch from third-man combinations to solo carries in five seconds.

Next, you build problem-solving resilience. The 8.5 is constantly solving spatial puzzles—when to hold width, when to invert, when to trigger a press, when to drop into the base. That kind of thinking can't be coached solely in theory. It needs live reps with variable conditions. Set up scenarios where the player has to interpret the opposition's shape and adjust their positioning on the fly. No coach instructions, no pre-set patterns. Just read, react, repeat.

Then you layer in psychological training. The all-phase midfielder doesn't just deal with complexity—they thrive in it. That means building mental stamina. Not just fitness, but cognitive endurance: the ability to make elite decisions in minute 89 with the same clarity as minute 5. Mindfulness training, visualisation, even chess and pattern recognition exercises are being used in top academies to sharpen this edge.

Leadership is part of the build, too. Not the armband-wearing kind, but the silent kind that governs tempo and shape. The 8.5 is often the player others move around. That means communication, even when you're not speaking—through body orientation, gestures, eye contact. Coaches need to develop this layer deliberately. Run training games where the 8.5 is in charge of setting the pressing trigger. Or have them manage the build-up cadence. Teach them to be vocal without shouting, to lead without dominating.

And finally, the modern all-phase midfielder must own their development. The most dangerous 8.5s are the ones who are obsessed with their craft—not for ego, but for evolution. They study tape not to admire their highlights, but to dissect their spacing. They ask for specific feedback. They train ugly—working on the weak foot, the wrong angle, the uncomfortable carry.

There's no shortcut to building this kind of player. It's a grind. A thousand micro-decisions, a thousand reps in the grey zones of the pitch. But when it comes together, you get a player who doesn't just function in systems—they elevate them. A player who doesn't just adapt to the game—they shape it.

That's where the game is going. Not towards specialists, but toward synthesists. Not robots, but readers of chaos. Not players who can do one thing perfectly, but who can do many things precisely when it matters. And that's the modern 8.5 in full flight.

Redefining the Game Starts with You

This is Just the Beginning

The 8.5 isn't just a tactical evolution—it's a mindset shift. If you've made it this far, you know this role isn't about a number on a lineup sheet. It's the connective tissue of modern football, the role that lives in the grey areas, where structure meets spontaneity and theory meets instinct.

You've explored how this hybrid emerged from the ashes of the classic No. 10, how it thrives in today's fluid systems, and how it bends traditional formations into tools of creative expression. But this isn't the end of the journey. It's the spark that lights the next chapter—for you, your team, your analysis, or your personal development as a player or coach.

Now, it's about what you do with this knowledge. Because football doesn't stand still, and neither should you.

The 8.5 Mindset: Think Like a System, Act Like a Disruptor

To truly embrace the 8.5 role, you need to think beyond individual actions. Great midfielders don't just play football—they interpret it. They read the context, adjust the tempo, and influence the geometry of the game without needing to be the biggest, fastest, or flashiest player on the pitch.

This role rewards those who think in systems. That means understanding how your movement affects others, how your positioning changes the passing map, and how your decisions alter the opponent's structure. The best 8.5s don't just follow instructions—they manipulate the matrix.

But it also demands disruption. You must break the opposition's rhythm, collapse their pressing triggers, and find space where others only see compression. The ball isn't your only weapon—your movement, your timing, your presence in the half-space or on the blindside is just as dangerous.

The mindset? It's part chess player, part street footballer. Think strategically, act instinctively. Don't just play within the system—bend it in your favour.

What Happens Next: Applying the 8.5 Lens to Your Game

Whether you're a coach, analyst, player, or just someone who obsesses over tactics at 2 a.m., the next step is applying the 8.5 lens to your daily football life. Here's how you can start doing that—today.

Break Down the Match Differently

Start watching games with a new set of eyes. Don't just follow the ball. Watch what happens between the lines. Look for players who drift into the half-spaces, who check their shoulder before receiving, who drop to create an angle then burst into the box unnoticed.

Track their positioning during transitions. Are they the first to press or the first to cover? Do they float wide to create overloads or hang centrally to split centre-backs with a late run? Are they involved in the third-man combinations or ghosting into pockets left by inverted full-backs?

Every match becomes a tactical case study. You'll start noticing how one player's movement can tilt an entire defensive block. That's the 8.5 effect. And once you see it, you can't unsee it.

Rethink Training and Development

If you're coaching or mentoring players, you now have the tools to develop the next generation of hybrid midfielders. Start building drills that replicate the chaos of real game transitions. Design exercises that force players to scan constantly, make decisions under pressure, and rotate through multiple roles within a single phase.

Focus on the in-between skills that rarely get isolated:

- Scanning under pressure before receiving
- Timing late arrivals into the box
- Delayed pressing triggers from midfield
- Rotational play between pivot and hybrid role

Football is no longer about specialists. It's about players who can switch gears in real time and master multiple responsibilities without losing clarity. That's what the 8.5 embodies. Train for ambiguity. Reward anticipation. Build players who think holistically.

Integrate Hybrid Thinking into Your Strategy

For analysts and systems thinkers, the next step is embedding hybrid thinking into your frameworks. Start mapping not just positions, but functions. Create heat maps that track influence zones, not just touches. Analyse passing chains that start from half-space occupations and end in final-third overloads.

Look at metrics that better reflect the hybrid role's value:

- Progressive carries under pressure
- Pre-assist involvement
- Defensive recoveries in transition zones
- Positional rotations per 90

The old stats don't capture the hybrid impact. You'll need to think in layers—like an architect designing a building that adapts to its environment. The 8.5 is about creating solutions within chaos. Your tactical frameworks should reflect that.

Your Role in Shaping the Future

Football's next revolution won't come from a single formation or a viral tactic. It'll come from minds that understand the game as a living system—fluid, volatile, and full of opportunity. The 8.5 is a signpost pointing towards that future.

But systems only evolve when the people inside them demand it. That's where you come in. Coaches who build players that can think in multiple dimensions. Players who see the game in patterns rather than positions. Analysts who challenge surface-level data and go deeper.

177

This book is your blueprint—but the real transformation happens when you apply it, tweak it, and make it your own. The 8.5 isn't just a role. It's a philosophy. A way of seeing football not as a set of positions, but as a network of relationships.

So whether you're preparing your next match plan, building your player development curriculum, or just watching your favourite club with a tactical eye, you now have a new lens. One that sees the invisible threads connecting every phase. One that recognises the future of football is already here—it's just wearing a different number on its back.

And if you want to go even deeper—whether that's refining your team's tactical approach, building a hybrid midfield profile, or developing a system that brings fluid roles to life—get in touch.

I work with coaches, clubs, players, and analysts who want to future-proof their football. If that sounds like you, head over to [www.rondofootball.net] and let's talk.

Because in football, as in life, the edge goes to those who adapt faster. Those who think deeper. And those who act before the game catches up.

Let's redefine the middle of the pitch—together.

Rondo Football

Rondo *football*

Thanks for Reading!

Seriously, thank you for taking the time to read this—it means a
   lot. If you're into football and love digging into tactics, systems,
   or just talking ball in general, I think you'll enjoy what I do outside of the book too.

Rondo Football

I run a YouTube channel called Rondo Football, covering the
   intricate narratives of the beautiful game and everything in

between. Check it out here: **www.youtube.com/@RondoYT**

Follow Along

You can also follow me on X (formerly Twitter): **@S7MU3L**—
and be sure to follow **@Rondofootball_** for updates, thoughts
on the game, and occasional live match reactions. Also, visit
our website: www.rondofootball.net

Let's Stay in Touch

If you enjoyed the book, be sure to check out my other work and
feel free to reach out or share your thoughts. And if you're up
for it, a quick review goes a long way to help others discover
it too.

Printed in Dunstable, United Kingdom

65693881R00111